THE POWER OF GOOD PEOPLE

SURVIVING
SRI LANKA'S CIVIL WAR

Praise for The Power of Good People

'I read a book about two islands, about the sea, about love and voyage, and about the will to survive pitched against brute human cruelty, Nature's fury, and indifference. I began to read with trepidation at the weight of the subject, and finished at a single sitting with the images of this storm-tossed Odyssey firmly fixed in my heart. Caught between the pincers of war forged in the logic of tit-for-tat brutality, there is only one direction if one is to escape the inevitable final clamp.'

Gordon Weiss, UN official, author of *The Cage: The Fight for Sri Lanka and the Last Days of the Tamil Tigers*

'An uplifting collaboration that reveals how random acts of kindness can turn a story of trauma, torture and tragedy into one of hope.'

Michael Gordon, award-winning journalist and former political editor of *The Age*

'Amid the polemics of the political debate about asylum in this country, it is too easy to forget that, at the very heart of this issue, lies not some political theory, some abstraction, but people. This issue is not about boats to be stopped nor borders to be protected, it is not about "illegals" jumping queues nor national security. It is about people. People like Para.'

Ben Doherty, immigration correspondent, *The Guardian*, former South Asia correspondent, *The Sydney Morning Herald*

'One of the most touching elements in this extraordinary story is Para's chance friendship with an Australian grandmother who takes him into her family. This book is a collaboration between them and a powerful example of how people can really connect across cultures, class, age and gender to do good where politicians and bureaucracies have failed.
I highly recommend it.'

Frances Harrison, author of *Still Counting the Dead:*
Survivors of Sri Lanka's hidden war

'Para Paheer's lived experience combines conflict, suffering, courage, tragedy, compassion, and hope. It depicts events that are predatory and abominable, even as it celebrates the humane and good. It must be read, precisely because it is heart-wrenching; because the discomfort it elicits may goad us to abandon apathy, embrace sympathy, and thereby discover our common humanity.'

Professor Neil DeVotta, Department of Politics and
International Affairs, Wake Forest University

'This is a deeply personal and moving story of human resilience, patience, compassion and gratitude. May it move others to empathy and provide insight into the desperate circumstances which force a person to flee their home and become a refugee. Accounts like these are so important in changing Australia's inhumane immigration policies.'

Senator Richard Di Natale, Leader of the Australian Greens

THE POWER OF GOOD PEOPLE

SURVIVING SRI LANKA'S CIVIL WAR

A refugee's remarkable journey, and those who made it possible

PARA PAHEER WITH **ALISON CORKE**

Published by Wild Dingo Press
Melbourne, Australia
books@wilddingopress.com.au
www.wilddingopress.com.au

First published by Wild Dingo Press 2017
Text copyright © Para Paheer & Alison Corke
The moral right of the authors has been asserted.

Except as permitted under the Australian Copyright Act 1968, no part of this book may be reproduced, stored in a retrieval system, or transmitted in any form or by any means, electronic, mechanical, photocopying, recording, or otherwise without prior permission of the copyright owners and the publisher of this book.

Cover design: Greg Jorss
Cover photo: Steve Hardie
Editor: Jackey Coyle
Typesetting: Midland Typesetters, Australia
Print in Australia by Ligare

National Library of Australia
Cataloguing-in-Publications Data

Para, Paheer, author.
The power of good people : surviving Sri Lanka's civil war
/ Paheer Para with Alison Corke.

ISBN: 9780648066323 (paperback)
ISBN: 9780648066347 (e-book)

Subjects: Pararasasingam, Paheertharan, 1978-
Civil war—Sri Lanka.
War victims—Sri Lanka.
Refugees—Sri Lanka—Personal narratives.
Sri Lanka—History—Civil War, 1983-2009—Personal narratives.

Other Creators/Contributors: Corke, Alison, author.

Paheertharan Pararasasingam (Para Paheer)

Following arrest, imprisonment and torture because of his student activism, Para escaped from Sri Lanka. He later fled from India with thirty-nine others, on a tiny fishing boat that sank in the Indian Ocean. In an extraordinarily brave rescue by a gas tanker, *LNG Pioneer*, twenty-seven asylum seekers were saved and taken to Christmas Island Detention Centre where they remained for nearly two years.

A friendship developed after Para started corresponding with Alison Corke, which later enabled his release into the community. In 2017, Para became a proud Australian citizen. Separated from his wife and son for eight years, Para hopes to be reunited soon.

Alison Corke

Alison Corke is a freelance writer, living in Apollo Bay, Victoria.

The plight of refugees and the increasing demonisation of innocent asylum seekers led Ali to join Rural Australians for Refugees and later to establish the Apollo Bay branch.

In 2009, Ali heard that a tiny fishing boat carrying asylum seekers had sunk in the Indian Ocean. Extremely affected by the human tragedy of this event, Ali had no idea that soon she would become penfriends with Para, one of the refugees from that boat. On his release from detention in 2011, Para was invited to live with the Corke family.

Ali and her family believe that we all have a responsibility to care for each other's children.

Disclaimer

This is a true story of a young man caught up in a civil war spanning nearly three decades. Every care has been taken to verify names, dates and details throughout this book, but since much is reliant on memory, some unintentional errors may have occurred. Most real names have been replaced with substitute names to protect people remaining in Sri Lanka who may be in danger of recrimination. However, their actions and speech are accurately recorded.

The Publisher assumes no legal liability or responsibility for inaccuracies; they do however welcome any information that will redress them.

We dedicate this book to people everywhere who have been affected by war, and to those good people who are helping them to find a peaceful place in this world.

During Sri Lanka's Civil War, many thousands of people were killed; whole families perished in aerial bombing raids and other attacks, and tens of thousands of people were displaced. Even now thousands of Tamils are prevented from returning to their lands and rebuilding their homes and lives in the northern and eastern parts of the island.

People who were arrested during and at the end of the war are still missing. Families are left wondering what happened to their loved ones. Many women were forced into being the sole breadwinner, because their husbands were killed or disappeared during and after the war. Their children struggle to survive. Orphanages were established to care for destitute children. Without their grown children to care for them, elderly people face difficult and uncertain futures.

Profits from the sale of this book will be donated to orphanages and charities nominated by and known to Para Paheer.

Thank you for your support.

ACKNOWLEDGEMENTS

Time for Para and Ali to say 'Nanri'

Writing *The Power of Good People* has provided us with a wonderful opportunity to thank those people who kept Para safe. And now we are able to thank more good people who have made it possible to share our stories with you.

Without Catherine Lewis and Wild Dingo Press, our story might still wait to see the light of day. Catherine's enthusiasm to see stories shared, and her competence in enabling so many authors to write about their experiences are already legendary; we feel fortunate to add ours to her collection. Editor Jackey Coyle calmly helped us to weave shocking experiences into a compelling narrative. We thank them both for their professionalism and support.

Julian Burnside is a staunch ally and wonderful advocate. If only people knew just how much he does. Combine Julian's wisdom and his energy with his exceptional kindness and generosity and he becomes a formidable ally. What would we do without him?

Lisa Hartley was there from the beginning in 2009, helping asylum seekers to find pen friends who could bridge the gap between new arrivals and their place in the community. Without Lisa, we would have never met, and we are so grateful for her work and her continuing encouragement.

We became friends with Kerry Murphy (D'Ambra Murphy Lawyers) when we responded in 2010 to his articles covering the terrible injustices perpetrated against asylum seekers. He soon became our immigration lawyer and has helped us along the complicated legal journey from asylum

Acknowledgements

seeker to citizen. Then, bravely, he set off with us again in endeavours to bring Jayantha and Abi to Australia. Knowing he travels this road with so many both reassures and saddens us—he does it so well, but why is it made so hard?

We wrote unsolicited letters to people we admire—Professor Neil DeVotta, Richard Di Natale, Ben Doherty, Michael Gordon, Frances Harrison and Gordon Weiss, asking if they would read our manuscript and maybe offer a comment or endorsement. Each replied within days, with firm support, suggestions, endorsements and encouragement. All are extremely busy people, experts and authors in their field, and we thank them unreservedly for their help.

And of course, we thank our wonderful families and friends who listened to us, sympathised with us, became infuriated alongside us and galvanised us to write and finish this book. And then tolerated us while we did it.

Finally, the time has come to especially thank those people without whom there would be no book, because without them there would be no Para (or twenty-six other Tamils who would also have perished in the Indian Ocean back in 2009).

To Captain Brzica, *LNG Pioneer* crew members and Andy Hill, General Manager of the MOL group that manages the *LNG Pioneer* we say, 'Thank you' and 'Nanri'.

Every day.

FOREWORD

This is a beautifully constructed book. It is unusual, because it is written in two voices.

The first voice belongs to Para (Paheertharan Pararasasingam). He is a Tamil from Sri Lanka. He came to Australia as a refugee, having suffered extraordinary hardships in Sri Lanka. His story is a painful one, and uncomfortably familiar to anyone who has read about the grotesque mistreatment of Tamils in Sri Lanka during the long struggle for Tamil independence. While the Tamil Tigers engaged in the sort of brutality which desperation produces, the Sinhalese government behaved in ways which are all too familiar when a despised minority fights for its independence: white vans, torture, disappearances, murders. All these were part of the Sinhalese armoury in a terrible civil war which ran for twenty-six years. Most of us will never know civil war. It is not the same as a war between nations:

'… life can never be normal during a war, particularly a civil war when people often don't know the enemy, and can't be sure of the friend.'

Para's voice gives a first-hand account of the events which shaped his life in war-torn Sri Lanka, and a horrifying account of the brutal treatment he received at the hands of police, when he was taken into custody, on no evidence at all. Anyone who reads his account of what was done to him would understand why he risked everything in a terrible voyage to Christmas Island, on the boat later identified as SIEV 69.

But the second voice is Alison Corke. Ali met Para by letter, while he was detained by Australia on Christmas Island.

Foreword

Ali Corke is a grandmother from Apollo Bay who for years has been actively involved in refugee issues. When Para was released from immigration detention, she and her family invited him to live with them. Together, she and Para have told his story. And she captures the essence of a refugee's story:

'All of us have one thing in common—we have survived only through acts of kindness and compassion.'

Every Australian who has accepted the government's dishonest rhetoric about 'boat people' should read this book, so they can understand the horrors which cause people to flee, to leave behind the only culture they know, to risk everything in a dangerous journey across the ocean. For years, the Australian government has tried to persuade the Australian public that boat people are criminals from whom we need protection. It is a lie. Many Australians imagine that boat people come here as a lifestyle choice, but the fact is that boat people risk everything in their attempt to find a safe place to live. The risks they take are a measure of the dangers they are fleeing; a measure of their desperation.

If every Australian could understand the dangers boat people are escaping, they might have a more generous attitude.

They might understand why Ali Corke has done so much to help Para.

They might be prompted to have a more generous attitude to people who come here asking for safety.

They might show kindness rather than indifference or hostility.

This book shows how acts of kindness, great and small, can shape people's lives.

Julian Burnside QC, Refugee Advocate

TABLE OF CONTENTS

Map of Sri Lanka	xvii

PART I — 1

Prologue — 3

1. The letters — 9
2. From invasions to civil war — 17

PART II — 31

3. Stormy beginnings — 33
4. A deadly situation — 44
5. The displacement — 56
6. The running — 67
7. Education and enterprise — 79
8. The road to university — 89
9. Study, activism and love — 100
10. Trouble stalks — 114
11. Work, marriage and strife — 122
12. The masked man — 131
13. The white van — 137
14. The lucky escape — 149
15. A baby and a business — 159
16. Nothing but trouble — 168

17.	Colombo to Chennai	181
18.	The decision is made	194
19.	The journey	203
20.	The disaster unfolds	214
21.	Lost at sea	226
22.	Heroes and villains	237
23.	Welcome to Australia	251

PART III   261

24.	The unfinished story	263

Epilogue	269
Memorial speech	274
References	275

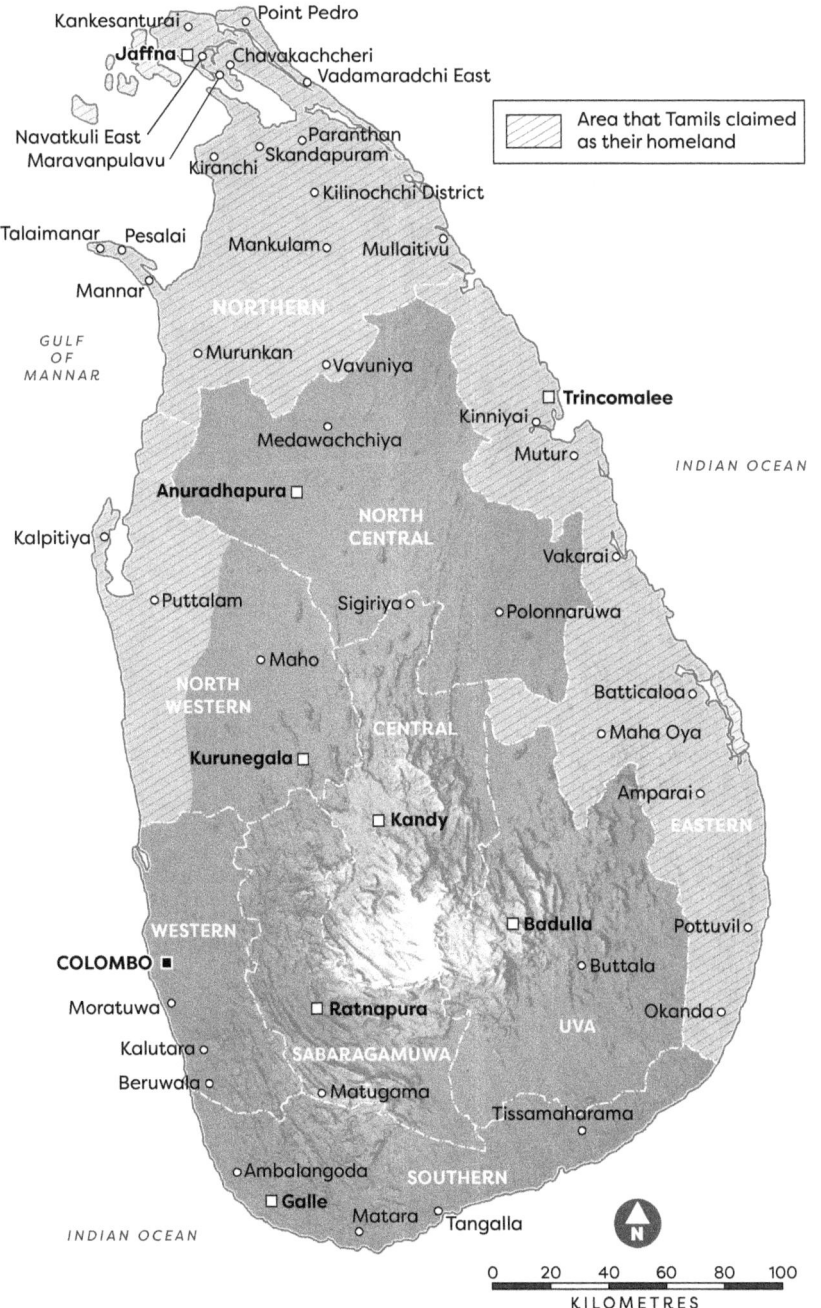

PART I

PROLOGUE

August, 2011. We sit quietly together. Darkness has fallen unnoticed and now, unless the fire flickers, I can barely see the young man across the room. I feel numb after hearing what he has just told me. He spoke first of poverty, hardship and adversity. He then shared stories of steadfastness, generosity and courage. Just now he told me of desperation, terror and torture.

I have no words. Just the age of my own children, he has experienced more horror in his thirty-three years than I could ever have imagined.

We are so silent and still that we can hear the first few raindrops pattering on the iron roof. I imagine them sliding down the window, like my tears. I find I am holding my breath, afraid to speak in case we lose this moment of shared stories, deep-rooted memories and profound, ongoing loss. When someone entrusts you with the events that have shaped their life, it feels like being handed a jewel—it must be protected, but should it be shared or locked away? What should I do with the information that has been so

Prologue

carefully, and at times so painfully, recalled and given to me?

I ask, 'What would you like me to do with this knowledge, Para?'

The rain falls more heavily. A log slips in the fire and the flames flicker, casting shadows in the soft glow. After a long, thought-filled silence, the young man shifts in his chair. I worry for him, revisiting those ghastly memories. I wonder what he will say next, now the demons of the past have been resurrected in his mind—but then, I doubt they ever really went away.

Another long silence ensues. I think he is struggling with what he wants to do with these recollections. I think along the lines of vengeance and anger and sorrow and wonder if he will ask me to just tell everyone how terrible his life has been. After so much suffering, what else can he want?

But I underestimate him. There is another long silence.

'I'm thinking back to everyone who helped me,' he finally replies. 'There are so many I would like to reach. I can never see them now, but I want them to know that I remember them and I am grateful. Some people helped me a lot, some people just a little. Many will not even know how they helped, but at the time it meant so much to me. Some saved my life. Some risked their own lives. One almost certainly died for me. I will never forget them. Please, will you help me to thank them?'

We both know that most of the people who helped Para would have little idea of the ripples that would flow from their 'unremembered acts'. Then again, several will remember the moment they played a part in helping him avoid hunger, or ridicule … or death.

Imagine if we could go back over our own lives and track down the people who influenced us in a way that was possibly small to them, but at the time was monumental for us?

A friend, now in her seventies, recently discovered at a school reunion that her high school English and French teacher was still alive. She immediately wrote to him, telling him that she remembered him as a compassionate and caring teacher who had a profound influence on her life.

'He knew I hated French and could not really master the subject, but I loved English,' Jane told me. 'I was a shy child, and spent most of my time reading in the school library. He would come to find me after exams and whisper, "Don't worry, Jane, I managed to find a couple of extra marks in your French paper. You've passed."'

Jane is now a highly regarded author and illustrator of exquisite and meaningful children's books, thus passing on the thoughtfulness once shown to her.

'I had always wished there was some way I could contact him to tell him that the bespectacled, shy student remembered him and his kindness, but by the time I realised the extent of his influence on me I had lost touch with the school, he had retired and I had no idea where to start looking. It was wonderful to write that letter to him—it was like a satisfying closure.'

Para feels the same way.

'I just want to somehow be able to say "thank you",' he says. 'I know that some of the people are dead now, but even so, I would like to mention them.'

If we are thrown into a life-and-death situation and someone rescues us, we are usually too intent on escape and survival to express thanks. All we can do is take the opportunity to say 'thank you' if the time ever comes.

There is another thing we can do—pay it forward.

Para is a living example of the philosophy of Stephen Grellet who was captured and sentenced to death during the French Revolution. After managing to escape to Amsterdam, he sailed to the West Indies. When he finally arrived in the United States, aged twenty-two, he could not forget the people who helped him avoid execution and escape. He became a Quaker and devoted the rest of his life to helping people across North America and Europe. These words are attributed to him, although others have claimed them, over the years:

> I expect to pass through this world but once; any good thing therefore that I can do, or any kindness that I can show to any fellow creature, let me do it now; let me not defer or neglect it, for I shall not pass this way again.

Having stared down hardship, terror, torture and death, Para now works tirelessly to help others, without expecting thanks. He supports close and extended family members in Sri Lanka and around the world—for example, when floods struck southern India in 2015, he was the first to find a missing cousin and then help him to re-establish his painting business. He sends money to help people still affected by the war, donates regularly to orphanages in Sri Lanka and India, and sponsors several children through World Vision.

But 'paying it forward' is not quite enough—through this book, Para wants to acknowledge and thank those who helped him.

'My life has been challenging at times, and I know that many others have had to cope with a much, much harder life than mine,' he says. 'We can all find ourselves in difficult places. If we are fortunate, a good person will care enough to help us. In helping someone, people discover they can do greater things than they ever thought possible. That is the power of good people. *Nanri*[1] is the Tamil word for 'thank you', and through this book I would like to thank them all.'

The world is a better place for having Para in it. And I have learned that we are more powerful than we realise.

So I begin this book saying *nanri* to Para—I feel honoured that he shared his stories with me and trusts me to help him to tell them. And *nanri* to all the good people who helped to keep Para safe.

---

[1] Pronounced 'Nandri'.

1
THE LETTERS

At the beginning of 2010, Dr Lisa Hartley was coordinating a letter-writing project supporting asylum seekers detained on Christmas Island. She wrote to all Rural Australians for Refugees members, asking people if they could make the time to write to asylum seekers in detention.

'Over the previous two decades,' she recalls, 'successive Australian governments had introduced policies aimed at deterring and punishing the arrival of asylum seekers. Since 1994, this included the policy of mandatorily detaining all asylum seekers who arrived in Australia without a valid visa. This policy saw thousands of people enduring long periods of detention before finally being accepted as refugees.

'After ten years of governance by the conservative Howard-Coalition party and the expansion of detention centres to remote areas in Australia and the Pacific, the election of the Rudd Labor Government in 2007 was met with cautious optimism by those concerned about the human rights of asylum seekers and refugees. However, with increasing numbers of boat arrivals in 2008, the Labor Government soon reinforced the indefinite nature of the mandatory detention policy and began to increase the number of Immigration Detention Centres. This included the expansion of facilities on Christmas Island, located in the Indian Ocean, 380 kilometres south of Java and 2650 kilometres northwest of Perth.'

The letter-writing project was established to bridge the gap between Australians and people seeking asylum, and to help asylum seekers improve their English. In November 2009, Dr Michelle Dimasi was living on Christmas Island, conducting field work for her PhD thesis. She established Asylum Seekers Christmas Island in response to the growing number of people detained there; it was difficult for mainland Australians to visit the detention facilities, and the detainees had a growing need for sustained advocacy about their rights. With very limited access to Internet or phones, they needed to know that many Australians supported and cared for them.

I thought this would be an ideal way of practising my skills—having a new Diploma in Teaching English as a Second Language—while helping someone improve theirs. I replied to Lisa and a few days later she sent a note with the name and email address of a young man with a long and interesting name.

In my first email, cautiously addressed to 'Mr Paheertharan Pararasasingam', I explained that I had been given his contact details by Lisa, that I was keen to help him improve his English through letter writing, and that I was an ordinary Australian person with a husband, three grown-up children and a granddaughter—lots of domestic detail because I didn't want him to be alarmed by letters from a complete stranger.

A few days later I received his reply, addressed 'Dear Madam'. He told me he had arrived on Christmas Island in November 2009, having been rescued by a huge gas tanker when his boat sank off the Cocos Islands after thirty or so days at sea, with the loss of twelve lives. His wife and son were left in India—he missed them greatly, but he had been forced to leave with the others on his boat because of persecution during the Sri Lankan Civil War and the ongoing danger of deportation back to Sri Lanka from India. He suggested I called him 'Para' rather than Mr Pararasasingam, apologised for any shortcomings in his English, and asked me to reply.

Para sounded pleased to have heard from me, so I replied, saying that I hoped we would enjoy being penfriends, that I was happy to help him with his English and that, since his own family was so far away, he might think of me as his 'Aussie mum'.

The next day, his reply pinged into my laptop—'Dear Mum …'.

Our journey had begun. I had no idea what extraordinary and at times, harrowing adventures were in store.

A lengthy exchange of emails followed—Para was in detention for nearly two years—until we finally met in August 2011. With daily practice, Para's English improved quickly. If he made a mistake, I would incorporate a correction in my reply. He absorbed the new knowledge expertly, looking up and writing down unfamiliar words and phrases, and if he could not figure out something, he would ask the detention centre staff.

The letters

I had no idea which subjects were off limits or if there were any culturally sensitive issues to avoid, but we muddled along. Our letters also shared news about each other's families, and I found myself looking forward to hearing from him each day. Sometimes Para did not have access to the computers in the detention centre, and then I worried about the silence and hoped everything was okay. Similarly, Para would worry if I was not in touch regularly, and when I told him I was travelling to India to catch up with my daughter he gave me lots of advice and seemed relieved when I arrived safely home.

I learned that Para had a wife, Jayantha, and a two-year-old son, Abilash. As the months passed, I learned about Para's extended family, the friends he had made in detention, the daily routines and the mounting frustrations. No one knew for how long they would be detained, if they would be assessed as refugees or returned to their country of origin, whether they would receive permanent residency, or even if they would ever see their families again.

They all longed to be allowed to settle in Australia and to bring their wives and children, but already Australia was tightening its grip on the borders, and we both saw that the official vocabulary was changing, with 'refugee' and 'asylum seeker' giving way to 'illegal immigrant' and 'illegal maritime arrival'—even though it was not then, and is still not, illegal to seek asylum.

Towards the end of his first year on Christmas Island, Para was sad and preoccupied, thinking about the twelve people on his boat who had drowned at sea. With help from some sympathetic staff members in the detention centre, he organised a memorial service, complete with service sheets. I had easier access to IT equipment, so together we prepared the content, then I emailed the documents to Para and he managed to get them printed.

I was beginning to realise that this modest and compassionate young man was also extremely intelligent and resourceful. Arranging an official memorial service in a different language from within a remote offshore detention centre that was split into several camps—and bringing together a number of detainees, case managers and church and other representatives—was no mean feat.

The service was attended by all the survivors—all were still in detention—and many staff. Para said it definitely helped them to cope with their personal situations, as they remembered those who had died, and reflected on their own good fortune in surviving. Even though they were still incarcerated with no idea when they may be released, they all had high hopes for the future.

Para's time in detention dragged on, with no end in sight. I started writing to anyone I could think of who might be able to intervene in his case, from ministers (state and federal, in government and in opposition) to case workers, refugee advocates, lawyers ... even the Inspector General of Intelligence and Security, the agency responsible for reviewing ASIO. No one was spared. It was frustrating and disappointing, but my letters led to lasting friendships with some remarkable and inspiring people.

After almost two years on Christmas Island, Para was transferred to Darwin Detention Centre. We began to plan for me to fly up there to meet him. Although he didn't really want our first meeting to be within the confines of a prison, it seemed to be the only way we would ever meet, as his detention seemed to have no end in sight.

One day I was passing the kitchen radio, arms laden with washing from the clothesline, when through the static, I heard the tail end of an interview with then Immigration Minister Chris Bowen. From memory, it went something like this:

INTERVIEWER: We are hearing that refugees are being held in detention for very lengthy periods, with no indication of when they will be released. Isn't it too harsh to keep them locked up like this?

MINISTER: Yes, they are kept in detention for health and security checks, but once they have cleared these, they could be transferred to live in the community, in a form of community detention.

INTERVIEWER: I suppose the problem there is that most will not know anyone living in the community, so won't be able to organise a placement?

MINISTER: That's true. If an asylum seeker could find a host family in the community, and they have satisfied the Department in terms of security and health checks, then they could move out of detention in a short space of time.

* * *

Since ABC Radio National reception was very poor in Apollo Bay back in 2011, it was extremely fortunate I heard the interview. Unceremoniously dumping the clean laundry onto the kitchen bench, I was back to my laptop in a flash, emailing Para's case manager to ask if community detention would be an option for him.

Fast forward a few months and many emails, phone calls and head-in-hands moments that included—for reasons we couldn't fathom—Para initially being flown to Brisbane, where he was placed for a few weeks while I negotiated furiously with the department to fulfil his wish to come to Apollo Bay.

My husband Charlie and I were standing with our daughter Georgie and her partner at the arrivals lounge in Melbourne Airport, waiting for Para to disembark.

I couldn't believe we had achieved this—after all those months in detention, Para was finally going to live in the Australian community, with a family. This would enable him to learn the customs, improve his language and relax away from the daily stress of imprisonment. He had been granted refugee status but so far, no visa, so he was not allowed to work, but at that stage we all felt he just needed some peace.

The doors opened and the ground staff cleared the way for the incoming passengers. Out lumbered an enormous man, the size and stature of a large grizzly bear. Georgie caught my eye—we had not seen a photo of Para, although we had sent him plenty of our family photos. Was this him? To my immense relief, the bear-man was quickly greeted by a person so similar that they could only have been brothers, and off they went.

Then a few businessmen emerged, ears glued to phones, racing to their next appointments. Some unaccompanied children bounced through the doors, shepherded by weary cabin crew. Families, couples and more singles followed; each time a young man appeared, Georgie would glance in my direction—with a cheeky half-smile if he seemed strange.

We had no idea what to expect. Had I done the right thing in inviting a stranger to live with us? But then, Para was not a stranger—our letters had been frequent and candid; I believed we already knew each other well—but I felt anxious.

The rush of people dwindled. There were a few seconds between passengers now. Where was Para? I began to worry—could the Department have changed its mind? Was he lost, or put back in detention somehow?

Finally, a few minutes later, at the end of the line, a young man of medium height appeared. His smile shone with exceptional brilliance against his dark skin. His eyes danced; he looked excited, hopeful and maybe a little uncertain.

I approached him tentatively. 'Hello, Are you Para?'

'Hello, Mum? Yes, I'm Para. Thank you for your letters. I think I will be fine now.'

2
FROM INVASIONS TO CIVIL WAR

I had many questions when I began writing to Para at the beginning of 2010.

Who were the Liberation Tigers of Tamil Eelam (LTTE): a terrorist group or freedom fighters? Were all Tamils LTTE members? Why was such a small country so ethnically diverse, with Sinhalese, Tamils, Muslims and other minorities? Why did so many people move around the country so often and with so little planning? How could Para, and so many others, have possibly come away, leaving a wife and baby behind? Why would someone even consider getting on a tiny, patently unseaworthy boat and embark on a six-thousand-kilometre ocean journey?

I gradually found answers in a litany of compelling and ghastly articles that frequently left me saddened and appalled. Then friends began to ask me the same questions—how could I explain?

So I turned to Para—the consummate teacher—and together we prepared a brief history. Although Para is Tamil and suffered extensively at the hands of the police and the

Sri Lankan Army, we have tried to present a fair summary to set the scene.[1]

If I had been able to access something similar at the beginning of our friendship, I may not have asked questions that in hindsight were possibly insulting.

Sri Lanka today

The island of Sri Lanka (known as Ceylon until 1972) lies about thirty kilometres off the tip of south-eastern India. It measures around 500 kilometres from its northernmost city, Jaffna, to Galle in the south.

Known as 'the jewel of the Indian Ocean' because of its shape, its beautiful beaches and its temperate highlands, Sri Lanka has deep harbours and a geographical location that made it extremely desirable to foreign powers. Its history is chequered by invasions and colonisation, with Portuguese (from 1505) and Dutch (from 1656) armies giving way to British occupation in 1796.

Today, the population of Sri Lanka numbers around twenty-one million. It is a country of multiple ethnicities, the two most prominent being Sinhalese (around 75 percent, with Buddhists among them amounting to 70 percent and concentrated in the central and southern parts of the country) and Tamils (around 13 percent, mainly Hindu and concentrated in the north-east). As well, there are around 10 percent Muslims (mainly Sunni) and 7 percent Christians (mainly Catholic).

According to a Gallup poll in 2008, Sri Lanka was the

---

1 See the references at the end of this book for further reading.

third most religious country in the world, with 99 percent of Sri Lankans saying religion is an important part of their daily life.

Diverse belief systems

The original inhabitants of Sri Lanka are said to be the Veddas, who are now a small population living in the central region. While Sinhalese and Tamils have both inhabited the island for hundreds of years, accounts about how and when they arrived in the country differ.

Some have argued that Sri Lankans are mainly from South India and that the Sinhalese became a unique community only after the spread of Buddhism and the development of the Sinhala language. In this telling, religion and language combined over time to give birth to a new ethnicity.

The Sinhalese, however, claim that they originate from an area that is now part of Bangladesh and that they were chosen by the Buddha to preserve his doctrine in Sri Lanka. In this telling, the Sinhalese Buddhists were chosen to protect and promote Buddhism, and Sri Lanka was also chosen as the repository of Buddhism.

Understanding this belief system is fundamental to understanding the divide between Sinhalese and Tamils, and why a political solution has eluded the island: because the Sinhalese now more or less believe that they alone are the 'sons of the soil' and minorities may be tolerated, provided they do not make undue demands.

Differing castes, religions and ethnicities have caused endless problems in Sri Lanka, exacerbated by the way in which the British governed and finally departed in 1948.

Colonial rule to independence

Nearly 150 years of British rule came with good and bad consequences.

Beginning around the 1830s, around one million Tamil speakers were brought in from India to work as labourers in the rubber and later, tea plantations. The economy flourished, but at the expense of the 'plantation Indians', who were forced to live like slaves under appalling conditions.

British and American missionaries established good schools in the northern (mainly Tamil) part of the island—then the British angered the Sinhalese majority by appointing Tamils to bureaucratic positions, because they now spoke good English. This 'divide and rule' policy was typical of most colonial efforts, and generally ended in tears, bloodshed and unspeakable horror after independence—such as when the Belgians left Rwanda, and the British left Sudan.

Nevertheless, the Sri Lankan independence crusade was a peaceful affair, especially when compared to what was happening in India. Tamils initially asked for more representation than their numbers justified and this led to some tension, but the Sinhalese and Tamil elites were able to cast aside their differences and amicably negotiate with the British. They thus accepted the constitution the British put together, which led to Ceylon being granted independence as the Dominion of Ceylon on 4 February, 1948. Twenty-four years later, on 22 May, 1972, it became the Republic of Sri Lanka.

Sinhalese and Tamil flashpoints

Unfortunately, on gaining independence, the Sinhalese majority began passing laws that discriminated against

Tamils. The first such law, *Ceylon Citizenship Act*, effectively banned plantation Tamils from citizenship, leaving around seven hundred thousand people stateless. The ancestors of these people had been brought out from India by the British more than one hundred years before, so they had nowhere else to call home. Sadly, caste considerations influenced many Tamils in the north to support the plantation Tamils' disenfranchisement.

The more offensive law passed by the Sri Lankan government was the 1956 *Sinhala Only Act*, which made Sinhala the only official language in state and public affairs and clearly discriminated against Tamils. The Sinhalese saw this as more of a levelling of the playing field, since Tamils had benefited from better education received during British rule, when schools in the northern parts of the island equipped students for university with professional qualifications and opportunities.

Tamil protests against the *Sinhala Only Act* led to the island's first anti-Tamil riots. Two years later, in 1958, government attempts to superimpose Sinhala lettering on vehicle numberplates led to more riots. Soon after, when the army was stationed in the north, Tamils came to consider this an occupation force. All this took place while Sinhala was being consolidated as the only official language and Tamils—who largely spoke Tamil and English, but not Sinhala—were being systematically eliminated from the civil service and other government positions.

Things did not improve—moving on to 1972, an educational standardisation policy required Tamil students to achieve higher scores to qualify for university than their

Sinhalese counterparts. And in a further affront, the constitution of 1972 conferred Buddhism as the state religion, ignoring Hindus, Muslims and Christians. Independent observers said these policies were designed to 'win elections' and while they certainly did that, satisfying the majority Sinhalese voters, they seriously offended Tamils, setting the stage for future conflict and encouraging a violent response.

A proposed solution

Throughout this time, member of parliament and former lawyer, SJV Chelvanayakam, was trying desperately to seek a peaceful solution to the growing ethnic tensions. He strongly opposed the culturally biased policies that were openly designed to offend, humiliate and subjugate Sri Lankan Tamils, even as he lobbied for a federal solution to Sri Lanka's ethnic problems. Sri Lanka's two main parties, on different occasions, came to agreements with Chelvanayakam, only to overturn them when Sinhalese nationalist forces protested. In hindsight, many of the ethnic problems that the island experienced could have been avoided if governments had stuck to these agreements.

By the early 1970s Tamil youth, frustrated by being systematically denied educational and career opportunities offered to their Sinhalese peers, began promoting 'Eelam'—a separate Tamil state. Even Chelvanayakam, whose peaceful campaigns led to comparisons with Mahatma Gandhi, realised that Tamils may be better off on their own if Sinhalese and Tamils could not resolve their differences.

Thus, by 1976, Chelvanayakam was leading a political

coalition, the Tamil United Liberation Front, and calling for a 'free, sovereign, secular, socialist state of Tamil Eelam'. He added, 'We have abandoned the demand for a federal constitution. Our movement will be all non-violent. We know that the Sinhalese people will one day grant our demand and that we will be able to establish a separate state from the rest of the island.'

Although Chelvanayakam died in April 1977, his legacy prevailed and three months later the party received 68 percent of votes in the northern province. Indeed, by 1977 it seemed that everyone knew a separate Tamil state was required. The General Secretary of the Tamil Eelam Liberation Front (MK Eelaventhan) observed, 'It is only in the creation of a Tamil state that a true spirit of friendship and cordiality could prevail between the Sinhala and Tamils on a permanent and everlasting basis'.

Could the whole dreadful war could have been avoided if this had been implemented?

No way forward

Seemingly, the growing call for a separate state would have caused Sinhalese leaders to try to accommodate Tamils' grievances. Instead, the governments in power in the 1970s pursued policies that further marginalised and alienated many Tamils.

In 1976 a young Tamil, Thiruvenkadam Prabhakaran, founded the military organisation the Liberation Tigers of Tamil Eelam—the feared Tamil Tigers. The LTTE aimed to create an independent Tamil state in the north and east of Sri Lanka using military force.

Professor Neil DeVotta, a political scientist specialising in South Asian politics,[2] observed that:

> The 1970s saw the situation in the north worsening, encouraging the rise of various rebel groups. By 1977 the Tamil United Liberation Front (TULF) had become the main opposition party yet the new government (the United National Party) failed to respond with policies acceptable to Tamils, despite many Tamils having voted for it. Even worse, the government allowed the racists in its midst to pursue anti-Tamil violence.
>
> The systematic growth of Tamil rebels shows that when a particular community feels it is being continuously terrorised by the dominant ethnic/religious or political group, many will join a politico-military movement to resist the oppression and violence of the persecutors,' he continued. 'This is the basis for the LTTE's [Liberation Tigers of Tamil Eelam's] rise and the legitimacy it enjoyed, notwithstanding the deadly brand of terrorism it cultivated.

The Jaffna Library burns

A civil war is generally not started by a single event. Instead, a multitude of factors occur over time until the situation is as unstable and flammable as a firework.

The first touchpaper was lit on 31 May, 1981 when three Sinhalese policemen were shot and killed during a rally held by the Tamil United Liberation Front. In response,

---

2 Prof. Neil DeVotta was born in Sri Lanka and, coincidentally, shares the same birthday as Para. After completing his secondary education at St Benedict's College in Colombo, he moved to the United States where he received a doctorate in political science and currently teaches.

the following day an organised mob of Sinhalese origin (including police and political operatives) went on a rampage through Jaffna; Tamils were dragged from their homes at random and killed, businesses and Hindu temples were destroyed and the day ended in the burning of the Jaffna Public Library. At the time, it was one of the biggest libraries in Asia, containing more than ninety-seven thousand books and irreplaceable, historic manuscripts.

Tensions were exacerbated by the government response—two cabinet ministers downplayed the event, saying it was 'an unfortunate event where a few policemen got drunk and went on a looting spree all on their own'. The incident went unreported by the national newspapers. Instead of apologies, Tamil politicians were told in parliament: 'If there is discrimination in this land ... then why try to stay here? Why not go back home to India? There are your temples and gods. There you have your culture, education, universities, etc. There you are masters of your own fate.'

Black July 1983

Conflict and ill-feeling grew, and it was only a matter of time until the next flame became an inferno.

On 23 July, 1983, the LTTE ambushed and killed thirteen Sri Lanka Army soldiers. Retribution was swift and deadly. The following night anti-Tamil pogroms began in Colombo and spread rapidly to other parts of the country. In the ensuing week, hundreds, maybe thousands of Tamils were killed (estimates vary from four hundred to three thousand); thousands of homes and shops were looted and destroyed, and one hundred and fifty thousand people were made homeless. Fearing the worst, many Tamils fled to other countries around the world.

Details surrounding the events of the following days are harrowing in the extreme.

Many observed that the events of Black July were not a spontaneous response to the ambush and thirteen deaths, but something much larger and more sinister. Two months after the riots, as Paul Sieghart of the International Commission of Jurists wrote in *Sri Lanka: A mounting tragedy of errors*:

> Clearly the July 1983 attack was no spontaneous upsurge of communal hatred among the Sinhala people—nor was it, as has been suggested ... a popular response to the killing of thirteen soldiers the previous day by Tamil Tigers. It was a series of deliberate acts, executed in accordance with a concerted plan, conceived and organised well in advance.

Eleanor Pavey, of the International Security Sector Advisory Team, wrote in 2008:

> The systematic and well-planned nature of the attacks against the Tamils ... ruled out the spontaneous outburst of anti-Tamil hatred within the Sinhalese masses. Moreover, the possession of electoral lists by the mobs—which enabled them to identify Tamil homes and property—not only implied prior organisation, for such lists could not have been obtained overnight, but it also pointed to the co-operation of at least some elements of the government, who had been willing to provide the mobs with such information.

Whether planned or spontaneous, Black July 1983 was the terrifying start of full-scale civil war in Sri Lanka between the government and Tamil rebels bent on secession. The twenty-six-year-long war continued as it began—ferocious, ruthless, relentless and unforgiving—and ended in unimaginable horror. No one survived unscathed; many people were maimed, some families were completely obliterated, most lost loved ones. Civilians were used shamelessly by both sides. In the north, people had to make monumental and generally impossible decisions, usually at a moment's notice, and the consequences of getting it wrong were generally dreadful.

Although acts of extreme bravery and generosity rivalled actions that were beyond wicked, it is hard to believe that people involved in such a war can ever fully recover from their grief and pain.

The end of Sri Lanka's Civil War

In November 2005, after more than two decades of daily horror and bloodshed on both sides, Prime Minister Rajapaksa was elected president with the promise that he would end the war.

Neil DeVotta observed: 'The LTTE ended up doing the Tamils no favours, given that it waged a war by demanding so much from them yet producing nothing to secure Tamil rights. And while the Rajapaksa government brought the war to an end, it did so by resorting to the most brutal tactics.'

In a 2017 essay, DeVotta noted:

> The day after the war ended, Sri Lanka's then President Mahinda Rajapaksa told parliament that his soldiers achieved victory by 'carrying a gun in one hand, the Human Rights

Charter in the other, hostages on their shoulders, and the love of their children in their hearts'.

The LTTE had used the very Tamils it claimed to protect as human shields, and the nearly three decades long conflict ended with more than three hundred thousand people fleeing from the LTTE-controlled areas to government-controlled areas. The military did assist some fleeing Tamils, and some possibly were carried to safety on soldiers' shoulders.

But this was no humanitarian operation. If anything, it was akin to what happened in Grozny when the Russian army flattened that city while combating Chechnya's rebels, and to what is now taking place in Aleppo, Syria.

For Sri Lanka's military wiped out the LTTE without differentiating between combatants and innocent civilians, going so far as to deliberately shell hospitals and the government's designated 'No Fire Zones'. And it thereafter killed and 'disappeared' numerous LTTE personnel and supporters who had surrendered even as it sent more than ten thousand LTTE cadres into rehabilitation programs.

The consequences of such scorched-earth counter-terrorism are now playing out, with a new government claiming to pursue reconciliation and accountability with the Tamil minority even as it fends off allegations of war crimes from the international community.

The United Nations estimates that more than forty thousand Tamil civilians died in the last days of the war. For detailed knowledge of events at the end of the war, look up the Channel 4 documentary *No fire zone*—it is a chilling recount of the final, brutal days.

The Sri Lankan government had cleared out all independent witnesses, leaving the defenceless civilian population at their mercy. Hospitals were targeted and shelled to the extent that the Red Cross was requested by the Tamils to stop sharing GPS co-ordinates with the army—the very system designed to protect civilians was turned around to destroy them.

Time has not been a great healer. Steve Crawshaw, Advocacy Director for Amnesty International, observed, 'I think it's difficult to calculate how great the consequences may be if we—the world—continue in the absolute failure to address the truth and horror of what has happened in Sri Lanka'.

As international human rights lawyer Professor William Schabas said, 'The unpunished crimes leave wounds that return and prevent societies from healing and moving forwards'.

The casualties of this terrible war were not just those who perished, but also those who have tried against all odds to rebuild their lives while dealing with everlasting trauma.

Para's story is one example.

PART II

3
STORMY BEGINNINGS

November marks the start of the rainy season in northern Sri Lanka, so the weather is likely to be wet, windy and wild. But 2 November, 1978 crashed in with a storm so fierce that coconuts were flung from their trees, rain swept away the sides of the mud houses and the woven palmyra leaves on the rooftops tore free and flapped madly in the wind.

This was the day that the gods chose for the baby Paheertharan to enter the world.

'When her labour pains started, Mum told Grandma, and she fetched my dad,' Para says. 'The weather was so wild that Dad knew the only way to reach the hospital was by car. In our village of Navatkuli East there was just one car, the taxi driven by Dad's cousin Nallaiah. Dad ran to his house and at first he was reluctant to drive anywhere in the storm, but when he knew that Mum was in labour, he agreed to come.

'There was no road by our house so Dad had to carry Mum on his back along the laneway between the paddy fields. They were stung by the rain and saturated from the dripping leaves; Dad felt the water rising quickly up his legs. Then luckily another cousin, Bala, saw them struggling and came to help. Between them, they managed to carry Mum down the lane and onto the road where they waved to Nallaiah, who drove up alongside them. The wind almost wrenched off the door when Bala opened it, but somehow they bundled Mum inside and set off.'

The road was slippery and full of potholes. They drove carefully between the paddy fields—a nerve-wracking ride because at any moment the vehicle could have slid off the slick, muddy road—until they reached Navatkuli Bridge, which crossed over the ocean. Huge waves smashed against the sides of the car, and the wipers struggled to keep the windscreen clear.

Eventually, they arrived at the hospital.

'Bala ran in ahead,' Para continues, 'only to be told they could not enter because of the rising floodwater. There in the entrance he held his ground and argued with the security officers until a guard finally allowed Dad to wade in, carrying Mum. The wards had been moved up to the second floor because of the floods, so Dad carried Mum all the way up the stairs. He took her straight into the delivery ward and the doors slammed shut behind her, blocking out the sound of the storm. At last, she was safe.'

Soon after, Paheertharan Pararasasingam—Para—entered the world. As her newborn son grasped his mother's finger, she could not have known what adventures, dangers, troubles and joys this little person was going to encounter.

Fast forward a few years. Para had grown into a happy, if perpetually hungry, little boy. He lived with his parents, grandmother, older brother Panneer and younger sister

Pugalini in a tiny mud house in their village, located in the northern part of Sri Lanka.

They were extremely poor and the three children always had jobs to do. Para doesn't remember many days spent playing.

'From being tiny I was always working to help my mum—finding firewood, sweeping the mud floors of our home, collecting coconuts and pulling weeds from the paddy fields,' he says. 'We had to get up early each day. My first job was to scoop water from the pond and water the coconut trees that surrounded the house, while my brother watered the plants in the vegetable garden. Then we had to rinse the pots and go to the well to fetch fresh water for cooking and drinking. My little sister had to put away the sleeping mats and sweep the dirt floor. There was very little food, but usually Mum managed to make us roti that she wrapped in paper and gave us to take to school.'

The kitchen area was built onto the outside of the house. Three small dirt mounds in the shape of a triangle were used to support the cooking pot, with a fire lit in the middle underneath. In this way, using just the single pot, Para's mother and grandmother boiled water, cooked rice and made curries. A few essentials—salt, sugar and oil—were stored in old milk-powder tins.

'It was a hard life,' Para recalls. 'My grandma spent much of the day sitting by the fire to keep it going and cooking rice and whatever we had for the meal. We ate at lunchtime, and then we saved some food for the evening. We never had meat, and usually we just had rice taken from the paddy field, mixed with scraped coconut and spices and sometimes vegetables from the garden. In the dry season the pond would dry up and then I could wade into the mud and dig down for lotus roots that Mum would scrape and fry. In the wet season, I was able to take my rod and fish in the pond. My sister liked fried fish, so Grandma would prepare this for her.'

The village did not have electricity, so in the evenings people used kerosene hurricane lamps and at night Para's grandmother tucked him alongside her in the outside kitchen, away from the fire so he didn't burn himself.

'My mum and dad slept together, in the room with my brother and sister, but I slept next to Grandma. She was always there for me. Much later, when I was living away at school or university, if she knew I was coming home to visit she would always stay up for me. No matter what time I arrived, even if it was in the middle of the night, I knew she would be there waiting patiently. She would blow on the embers to start the fire, then heat up some rice or curry she had saved for me. I loved her so much, and she loved me too.'

The village was home to Para's father's family. Thirteen brothers and sisters meant lots of uncles and aunties and many, many cousins. Para's father was much poorer than his siblings, making the early days difficult for Para.

'Sometimes I would go to their houses on the other side of the village,' he says. 'Usually I was not even allowed inside, and if I did enter I was told not to touch anything. They had so much more than we did, but they were selfish and often mean. Seeing me fishing in the pond for food, my cousins would laugh at me. We were poor, but we still had our pride. Grandma and Mum would tell me to ignore them and, even when they were cruel, to make sure that I was always kind.'

Para's grandmother told him, 'Do not get angry with them. One day you will have something that they do not, and when that happens, you should give it to them. Then they will know how it feels to be given something you really want.'

Para started school in 1985. Navatkuli Maha Vidyalayam in Jaffna had around fifteen hundred pupils from preparatory grade to Year 12, with more than a hundred and twenty pupils in each class. Discipline was rigid but reasonably fair.

Para was very bright, but his early days at school were made more difficult by his poverty.

'I was the very poor child with the faded, threadbare clothes,' he says. 'My shirt was worn out, it was paper thin, and my blue school shorts were almost white after so much washing. Poor Mum, she worked so very hard, and earned only a pittance, around fifty rupees [about eighty cents] a day. This meant we could not afford to buy many clothes and my brother, sister and I had only one uniform each, so Mum washed them by hand every day and spread them out to dry in the sunshine. We couldn't iron anything, and the school's discipline teacher, Ragupathy, often commented on my crumpled appearance. I frequently felt ashamed, and the other students would sometimes tease me. All the families in our area were poor, but our family must have been the poorest in the village. We did not even have enough pencils and paper.'

Para's father was strict and demanded absolute obedience from his wife and children.

'I remember one evening we children were studying in our house when we heard a strange noise and lots of laughter, so my brother, sister and I followed the sounds and

Stormy beginnings

at the other end of our village came to a house with a small television sitting outside on a table, surrounded by children and adults all sitting on the ground. We had never seen a television, so we sat down with the others and watched. It was wonderful.

'Soon it grew dark and my sister fell asleep on my knees. We knew we should not have been there, and if Dad found out we would be in terrible trouble. My brother Panneer became worried and said he was going home with our sister before Dad saw us, but I was glued to the screen. I now know we were watching *Tarzan* and I couldn't tear myself away. I thought it would be okay to stay—we'd never watched television before and I loved watching Tarzan calling and swinging through the trees to sit beside the wild animals. I was totally engrossed.'

The seven-year-old Para did not see his father standing outside the flickering circle. But when the show was over, he felt a heavy hand on his shoulder as he was leaving.

'He was furious. He dragged me back to our house and tied my hands to the palmyra tree, then he took a stick and beat me. He told me he was disappointed in me, that I should have been studying because if I did not study I would never get anywhere, that I had let him down, that I could not be trusted—he had thought I was doing my homework. On and on he shouted while he hit me. Grandma came to my rescue and tried to get between us, but he told her to leave. It was awful.'

A few days later, Para was completing his homework when he heard Tarzan's call ringing across his make-believe jungle and through Para's real-life village.

After the last beating, could he ignore Tarzan's call and the temptation?

'No. Dad was not at home, he wouldn't catch me, so I ran back to the television and sat watching it. Then out of the corner of my eye I saw my dad. Our eyes met and he left. I felt quite sick—the last beating had really hurt. I couldn't enjoy the show any longer, so I went home. Dad was there. Grandma's eyes were wide, Mum's also. My sister hid and my brother found some work to do. I was expecting a real thrashing this time.'

But his father ignored him. Time passed.

'My hands were sweating, I kept swallowing anxiously. I was really scared. Then Dad just told me to sit down with him.

'"Para," he said, "I beat you last time because you disobeyed me and because I wanted you to know that school is the most important thing. If you waste time watching *Tarzan*, you are not studying." He gestured with his arm. "Look around you—this is poverty. We are all poor here, no one goes to university, no one has a good job. We all work from dawn to dark, just making enough to survive. You have a good brain; if you work hard, you can break out of this."

'He raised his hand and I flinched, but again it was just to gesture—this time showing the empty shelves of our kitchen, the empty kerosene tin, the broken palmyra leaves on our roof. "Go and watch *Tarzan*. Watch as much television as you want. And stay here, living like this."

'I never went back to the television. Dad was hard, strict and often brutal, but in that evening, he taught me an important lesson.'

Para needed light to study during the long tropical nights, but with no electricity in the area, they used kerosene lamps. 'We only kept one lamp at the house because we could not afford more kerosene. Each evening we would quickly eat our dinner, then my mother would give me the lamp while I studied. I only had two or three hours before the kerosene ran out, then if I was lucky I would study by the light of the moon.' But on cloudy nights, he had to wait until sunrise.

'We were always hungry,' he says. 'Sometimes it was hard to study because my stomach felt so empty. Then Mum would make a small fire and boil the pot, and we would drink black tea. We couldn't afford sugar, but Mum would sometimes bring hard brown toffees called jaggery that were wrapped in pieces of paper, and we would put these in with the tea. Then I would read and study by firelight, moving away from the flames when it was too hot, and shuffling back along the ground when I needed to see words more clearly.'

Every morning, Para walked to school with his sister after the chores were done. Most of the students rode their bicycles, some of them teasing Para as they passed, so to avoid them Para and Pugalini walked through the Neniyan Kulam paddy fields, hoping no one would see them.

But someone did notice them—the school principal, Muthulingam.

'We could have been invisible to him—poor children with nothing, not even a pencil—but he was the sort of man who saw potential in every child, whatever their caste, whoever their parents were, and wherever they lived.'

Muthulingam saw the boy's potential and how much he wanted to succeed, and he decided to help him to start climbing out of the poverty trap. Towards the end of his primary schooling, recognising Para's determination, potential and natural leadership skills, Muthulingam appointed him a school prefect.

Para says that becoming a prefect was one of his proudest days. 'One of the prefect's jobs was to lock all the doors at the end of each day, then hand the keys to the principal. When it was my turn, instead of letting me walk all the way home after I had completed the prefect's tasks, Muthulingam would give me a lift on his motorbike. I remember those two privileges so well—he put me in a position of trust, then he gave me a ride home. To a poor boy from the wrong caste, these actions meant so much. Lots of people remember a particular teacher who helped them—for me, Muthulingam was that teacher.'

Muthulingam also encouraged Para to participate in public-speaking competitions, debates and story writing.

'His encouragement gave me the confidence years later when I reached university, to join the student union and then to become the president,' Para says. 'Then there was the discipline teacher, Ragupathy. He was also the sports teacher and he urged me to join the soccer and cricket teams. We were all crazy about cricket and I was proud to represent the school as captain of several sports teams.'

The dark shadow of civil war was never far away, though. The Indian Peace Keeping Force (IPKF) had been called in by the Sri Lankan government in 1987 to help overcome the Tamil Tigers (LTTE), which had been formed in the mid-1970s to fight for Tamil rights. The IPKF soldiers were notoriously cruel towards Tamils. In 1988, Para was nine when they came to his home and took his father to their camp for questioning because they suspected him of being an LTTE sympathiser. After beating him, they found he was a government worker, so they released him.

'My dad was lucky,' Para says, 'but in the time the IPKF were in Sri Lanka they rounded up and killed hundreds of innocent Tamils.'

Most Tamils were glad to see the back of the IPKF when they were withdrawn in 1990, but after they left, people who were accused of working for them were in turn shot by the LTTE.

'People were shot without real evidence,' Para reflects. 'Life seemed to be so cheap.'

He remembers hearing a commotion one day when he and his sister were walking to school.

'We followed the people down the street and there at a junction we saw a young man we recognised, about twenty-two years old, sitting on a chair, surrounded by LTTE soldiers with guns. His hands were tied tightly behind his back with rusty wire. He was so scared, his knees were shaking together. People were either pointing at him, accusing him and shouting, or they were crying. Women were holding their hands over their faces. His mum was there and she was begging everyone for help, pleading for his life. He had a sign around his neck that said he was a traitor. They were saying he informed to the IPKF, but I don't think he could have; he was too young.'

There was a massive bang. 'The chair tipped over backwards and crashed to the ground and he was lying there in the dirt, dead. There was blood everywhere. His mother was wailing and holding his body, while trying to untie his wrists.

She was covered in his blood. There was so much shouting, it was hard to know what to think or who to listen to.'

Para and his sister were so shocked that they grabbed each other and ran home to tell their mother. 'She was very sad and just held us tightly.'

Another time, walking to school together, they found the gates were closed.

'We looked up and saw two heads were stuck on spikes, just by the gates. They looked strange and terrible, and they were smothered in flies. The eyes were open, though, and they seemed to be staring right at us. Again, we raced home, our hearts beating. I still don't know who those people were, or why they had been killed.'

4
A DEADLY SITUATION

Thirteen-year-old Para was in Grade 8 when he was invited, along with a few other students from his class, to attend the Maaveerar Naal (Heroes' Day) celebrations at a village some 10 kilometres away.

The first LTTE cadre had died in combat on 27 November, 1982. Five years later, Maaveerar Naal was declared to recognise this and to remember all LTTE members who died in action. By 1991, the days leading up to Maaveerar Naal were included in the commemoration and 'Great Heroes' Week' involved meetings, religious rituals and processions. Schools and villages organised events, inviting families to gather to mourn their dead relatives. The culmination of the commemorations was a function at which the LTTE leader, Prabhakaran, would speak, addressing Tamils around the world.

The prospect of visiting a large town was too exciting to pass up, even though Para's father was against the idea—it could be dangerous, he said.

'We hardly ever went anywhere, so it was an opportunity to explore outside our village,' Para says. 'We travelled by bus. We arrived and lined up in the hall of the school; I was at the entrance, offering flowers and sandalwood to the families as they arrived.'

Para was saddened to see all the grieving relatives, but it was good to remember those who had died.

After dinner, a musical program included dancing.

'Then above the sound of the music I heard the thrumming of heavy engines,' he says, 'then massive blasts and almost immediately the whole area was engulfed by smoke. Government planes had shelled the area, knowing there would be many Tamils gathered for the ceremonies.

'Everyone just ran for safety, but I had no idea where to go—this was the first time I had visited this village; we had been brought across in buses, and I didn't know the way home. People and children were running everywhere, screaming, and many were covered in blood. I kept stopping people to ask for directions, but everyone was panicking and no one could help me.'

Finally, he saw some other students in his school's uniform and they managed to find their way back to their village, arriving home around 10 p.m.

'My mum and grandma were so worried; they had heard about the attack, but since we didn't have phones there was no way to find out what had happened to me. They held me and cried with relief, and told me Dad had been out looking for me for hours. He had gone to the hospital in Jaffna to see if I was among the most seriously injured people, and he had searched for my dead body around the village where the bombs had fallen. I was touched to know he cared so much.' Then he arrived home and saw Para.

'He was absolutely furious and beat me so hard with a big stick. "I told you not to go!" he shouted. "You are always causing trouble. We have been worried about you." Now I am older, I appreciate he was beating me from fear and relief, but at the time I just didn't understand him.'

The civil war was confusing for everyone, especially children; it was hard for them to know which way to turn, and who was the enemy. On the one hand, the Sri Lanka Army soldiers were dangerous and frightening to Tamils, but the LTTE soldiers—the Tamil Tigers—could be as deadly.

'Around 1990 the LTTE wanted to build up their forces,' Para says. 'The soldiers would come to the schools on their bicycles and talk to the principals, who then had to let them speak to the Year 9 and 10 students, aged around fifteen or sixteen. I was only about twelve years old, but often I would slip in with friends and we would hide at the back of the hall and listen.

'It was like a roadshow—they would screen short films showing violence in Somalia, Ethiopia and Vietnam, then tell us how the Vietnamese all took up arms and managed to beat the most powerful country in the world because they were all united. Then at the end of the meeting they would ask students to raise their hands if they wanted to join them.

'It was almost kidnapping, but they made it look like fun to be a Tiger—they brainwashed many students. But when the families heard the Tigers were at their local school, they would come running to save their children and stop them from joining up.'

The LTTE soldiers were also visiting the villages and inviting older boys to join their cause. Later, girls were targeted as well. Many teenagers were lured by thoughts of independence, freedom and excitement, but most parents were terrified for their children's safety and did everything in their power to stop them from joining the rebel forces.

Countless families were split as parents desperately tried to take their older children out of harm's way, and it was around this time that Para's parents decided they should move his brother Panneer away from the danger of being conscripted by the Tigers. They knew it would be hard to manage without his father's wages—they were already so poor. But they all decided that their elder son's life was more important. In April 1992, Panneer and his father set off on the dangerous journey to Colombo, leaving fourteen-year-old Para, his sister Pugalini, his mother and grandma to fend for themselves.

'People who did not live there in those times often ask me, "Why did your dad leave you to look after your mum, sister and grandma on your own? What was he thinking?"' Para reflects. 'But people who knew what was happening then never need to ask. We just did what we could to keep each other alive.'

Once in Colombo, Para's father and brother tried to find work to support the rest of the family, but they themselves were struggling. Jobs were very hard to come by in the middle of the war, and the mainly Sinhalese community tended to be suspicious of employing Tamils. Frequently no money came from Colombo, leaving the family to scrape by with whatever they could earn and, every month, his grandmother's pension.

'Once each month Grandma was entitled to collect her pension. The office was more than five kilometres away, and she was old and frail, but she was a proud and determined lady and together we would walk, and walk, and walk—very slowly, but never stopping. We would finally arrive at the office and queue for over an hour and in the end she was given her pension money. And then we would walk all the way home again. Her pension amounted to a hundred and fifty rupees—much less than two dollars in Australian money. But a hundred and fifty rupees went a long way then, and she definitely helped us to survive.'

The civil war waged back and forth, with atrocities committed by both sides. In July 1991, the LTTE launched a massive attack at Elephant Pass—strategically important because it linked the Vanni district to the Jaffna peninsula. The battle was particularly violent, with fierce fighting lasting for many days, and heavy losses sustained by both the army and the LTTE.

Jaffna was the only hospital with the facilities to take the wounded, and the journey from the battleground was fraught with danger as the army and air force continued attacking the convoys of injured soldiers. The LTTE commanders ordered Para's school principal to send five hundred students to help, so everyone from Year 9 upwards was brought in to serve meals, distribute clothes and keep the roads clear to allow the convoys through.

'All along the main road—it was called the A9—students were told to stand about fifty metres apart, and we were all given a red flag and a green flag. When an ambulance was coming, we had to clear the road and wave the green flags, but if we heard planes coming in for a strike we had to wave the red flags so the ambulances and trucks carrying the wounded could get off the road and hide in the jungle. We were all scared—we were so young, but that was the reality of our lives. And the principal had no choice; he had to send us. You just did not argue with the Tigers.'

* * *

In November 1992, the army attacked Para's village with a supersonic jet. The bomb missed their home, but many people were killed.

'This was one of the first times they used supersonic planes, travelling faster than the speed of sound,' Para says. 'We could not hear them coming, we just suddenly heard and felt the enormous blasts. Mum screamed to me, Grandma and my sister, and we ran away from our house through the paddy fields to the Hindu temple—we thought it would be the safest place.

'At first, we didn't know it was an attack, because we hadn't heard the planes coming. When things quietened down, we returned to the village. People were walking around dazed, and some were bloody. We asked people what had happened. They told us there was a massive crater at the junction near our village and I asked Mum if I could go to see it. Of course, she said no, but still I went with my friends.

'When we arrived, we found LTTE soldiers were already there, checking the area to work out what sort of bomb it was. All around was devastation, with trees flattened and huge holes in the ground, bigger than the village pond. It horrified me to think what would happen if these bombs landed on our houses, but there was nothing we could do to prevent disaster. This was normal life for us, and for millions.'

A deadly situation

In December 1994, when Para was sixteen, he was confronted by an even more terrifying prospect—Ordinary Level (O Level) examinations.

'At that time, I was feeling so worried,' he says. 'My classmates seemed to have everything—bicycles, pens, notebooks and textbooks. I could not see how I could possibly compete with them. And the worst part was, they all attended a private tuition centre, so if they were weak in any subjects, they could ask their tutors for help. Everyone was determined to succeed—we all knew the only way to a better life came with a good education and success in school. The competition and the pressure were enormous.'

Para's family barely had enough to eat; they certainly had no money to spend on private tutors. One day, although embarrassed to ask for anything, Para plucked up the courage to approach his school principal. Muthulingam listened kindly, then he asked Para which subjects were troubling him. While he could not organise for Para to have private tuition, he could speak to the teachers at school, and he arranged for them to help Para.

'All the teachers took the time to sit with me and help me revise. I am forever grateful to Muthulingam—if he had not asked them to help me I would really have struggled in those examinations. I would love to find him and tell him what a difference he made to my life.'

Some years later when Para eventually became a teacher himself, he tried to work in the same way as his teachers had, always looking out for the poorer children who needed extra help and confidence.

There was another special teacher—the strict and

demanding Subramaniyam Iyar, who taught English. It was customary for the boys to sit at the back of the class, with the girls in front. But on the first day of term all the boys were told to sit at the front, close to the teacher where they could be watched.

'Subramaniyam Iyar knew I came from a very poor, low-caste family, but he didn't seem to mind,' Para says. 'He took a special interest in me, and even invited me to his house to study. He personally helped me so much. Maybe my teachers have forgotten their actions of kindness and generosity to a poor student; maybe they did not know how much they helped me to not only survive, but to learn and to do well. They gave me faith in myself, and they gave me the tools to do well at school. I think of them often, and thank them from my heart.'

Para didn't know then that one day in the future his life—and the lives of nearly forty others—would depend on his ability to communicate in English.

The tiny household was now really struggling to survive. Although his father and brother tried to send money from Colombo, they frequently had none to spare. Para's mother would take any job she could find, from cleaning houses to hard menial work in the fields, weeding rice paddies or mending fences. As soon as he finished school each day, Para would be working alongside her.

'Sometimes I discovered that we were working at the homes of people in my class at school,' he says. 'I remember that one day we were building a fence at someone's house, and the daughter came out to bring us tea. I looked up and saw that the girl was one of my classmates. I was embarrassed because I was working in the garden, and I worried what would happen at school next day. But she smiled at me and said, "Thank you for your work here. I won't tell anyone." I will always feel grateful to that girl for her kindness—no one wants to be so different in school. It was hard to be poor, and not many people supported us.'

But there was one relative who looked out for the little family, a kindly widowed aunt called Thankamma. Her husband, Para's father's older brother, had been a bus driver who was shot dead by the army.

'There was no reason for this,' Para says. 'The soldiers just drove by his bus one day at the depot. He was sitting with my other uncle, having his lunch. They shot him for sport. Things like that happened all the time.'

Thankamma had four sons and two daughters, but most of them had left Sri Lanka because of the war. Except for one daughter, they now all live in England.

'She really helped us,' Para recalls. 'For instance, if we were invited to a wedding or any special family event, we never had anything we could wear, so Thankamma would come to our house and lend clothes and jewels to Mum, and give me her son's shirts and pants. After the wedding, we would wash and return everything. If I passed her house she would tell me to wait while she cooked some fresh food for me to take home. It was tragic that she lost her husband, but it never made her bitter.'

Unlike another aunty, Nallamma.

'One day, my mum was very sick with something like the flu. Dad was away in Colombo and Mum was working so hard to try to earn enough money just to feed us one meal each day. I came home from school and found her sitting in the kitchen, crying because she was exhausted and unwell. I wanted to make her some hot sweet tea but we didn't have any sugar, and there was no money. I had seen my aunt Nallamma buying some sugar when I passed the shop on my way home, so I went to her house and asked if we could have a little sugar for my mum's tea because she was so sick. Nallamma was very rude—she told me she did not have any sugar at all, and I should go away.

'Luckily on the way home I found a coconut on the ground, so I took it to an uncle's shop and swapped it for a little sugar—it came in small packets of twisted paper. Then I went home and we made Mum some hot tea with sugar. She was very grateful and was sipping it while I told her and Grandma about Nallamma's selfishness. We three were sitting on the floor in the kitchen, with our dog Tiger between us, looking from me to Grandma and then to Mum as if he was listening to us. Later Mum said she felt a bit better, and we all went to bed.

'The next day there was an enormous commotion from Nallamma's house, with a lot of shouting and banging, so I went to see what was happening and found Nallamma screaming that wild dogs had come in the night and dug into her kitchen, smashing everything, breaking bottles and upending tins of powdered milk, flour and chilli powder. "It knocked over the sugar tin, and sugar is all over the floor and in the dirt—everything is wasted. I want to find that dog and kill it!" she yelled.

'I said, "But Aunty Nallamma, you told me yesterday that you didn't have any sugar …"

'She looked at me so angrily that I thought it time to run away. I told Grandma. She laughed and laughed and called Tiger to say, "Good dog, clever dog". He was dancing around us, wagging his tail. We were not totally positive that it was Tiger who had destroyed that kitchen, but I think and hope it was him.'

The time came to sit the O Level examinations. 'During the day of general examinations, it was usually very quiet with no shelling or fighting conducted by the LTTE,' Para says. 'But the Sri Lankan army kept on bombing and shelling the Tamil area. The Tamil students had to sit the general examinations, otherwise we couldn't get a chance to study higher education. Some Tamil students were killed in the examinations by Sri Lankan army shelling.'

Simply attending school each day and helping to provide enough food for the next meal was a huge daily challenge, but when the O Level results came out in 1994 Para was delighted to find that he had done extremely well. His cousins—particularly those who had mocked him for being so poor—did not manage such good scores, and some of them even failed. Para recalled a sense of pride when these cousins asked him to tutor them for the re-sits, although this was short-lived.

'I started teaching them—it was so nice that they had to finally stop looking down on me and needed my help. I became their teacher, and they paid me to tutor them. But when I gave the money to Mum she asked where it had come from and when I told her, she was furious: "Give it all back at once, you will not take money from your cousins!" I know she was right now, but at the time I was very unhappy. Anyway, I returned the money and continued tutoring them for no pay, and realised that I enjoyed teaching—this was when I decided I would like to study and become a teacher.'

But before Para could return to school to study for his Advanced Level (A Level) examinations in preparation for university and a career in teaching, another terrible event shook the Tamil community and set off a chain reaction that continued for the next fourteen years.

5
THE DISPLACEMENT

For many months, the civil war had been raging in the north of the island. LTTE soldiers would attack the Sri Lanka Army, and the army would retaliate. The impact on the civilians who happened to live in these areas was profound. Deaths and horrific injuries from shells, bombs and shrapnel were mounting. Many thousands were driven from their homes—Para and his family were not exempt, moving not only once but many times, both during and after the war.

The Sri Lanka Army was shelling from Palali and each Tamil's house had a bunker where the entire family quickly moved when the army shelled or bombed. Once the attack was over, they returned to their normal routine.

Para dug an L-shaped bunker in front of their house. 'When the army started shelling,' he says, 'then my mum, grandma, my sister and myself all moved into the bunker. Sometimes we had to stay the whole night until the Sri Lankan army stopped shelling. My mum always packed some clothes for everyone, and those two bags were always in front of the house, in case we had to move from our village.'

The fighting continued back and forth, then the army launched a new offensive in July 1995.

Operation Leap Forward was intended to strike down the LTTE and clear them out from the north. Thousands of innocent civilians lived in the area, and they were advised by the Sri Lankan government to seek shelter from the intense fighting in temples and churches, which were generally avoided during attacks, and so were thought to be safe. When the Sri Lanka Army dropped millions of leaflets telling people to move quickly, hundreds of men, women and children ran to seek sanctuary in the Church of St Peter and St Paul in Navali, near Jaffna town, which was thought to be a safe distance away from the battle lines. The Catholic church, school and grounds were packed with people who were terrified by the sounds of shelling and relieved to be safely inside the confines of the 'safe area'.

Sadly, their confidence was misplaced. On 9 July, 1995, the Sri Lanka Air Force bombed the packed church and school, killing more than a hundred and twenty people, predominantly women and children, and injuring many more. According to *Time magazine*:

> After hundreds of civilians heed the Sri Lankan Army's advice to seek refuge in St Peter's church at Navali, an air force plane bombs the building, killing more than 120 people ... Operation Leap Forward began at dawn on July 9 and the military warned civilians to clear the south-west of its base at Palali, recommending churches and temples as shelters. At 4.30 p.m.

a Pucara fighter plane flew towards the Navali church, three kilometres outside the combat zone, and bombed the sanctuary and adjacent courtyard.

Most of the people huddled inside were women and children, many of whom were killed immediately. Others had limbs blown off. Survivors were brought by tractor to the town of Jaffna six kilometres away, but the Jaffna Teaching Hospital and its lone surgeon weren't prepared. They soon ran out of bandages, antibiotics and beds.

'The treatment was crude,' said Subramaniam Jebanesan, the Protestant Bishop of Jaffna, who rushed to the hospital to help, '… limbs that could have been saved had to be amputated.'[1]

The International Committee of the Red Cross confirmed the massacre, reporting that thirteen babies were among the dead found under the rubble.

In the months following this outrage, aerial bombardments of civilians by the Sri Lankan government forced three distinct waves of refugees from villages in the north to flee to Jaffna, the country's second-largest town. The city was packed with displaced people, and government embargoes on food, water, electricity and communications had left people starving, as well as terrified by the constant shelling.

Operation Riviresa—the move to take over the city of Jaffna—began on 17 October, 1995. Forty thousand government troops and tanks advanced towards the city. Two weeks later, with just a few hours' notice, the Sri Lanka Army moved from its camp at Palali and started shelling Jaffna.

---

1 *Time*, 31 July, 1995.

Residents were ordered to move south to the area called Thenmaradchchy, where Para's village was located. As the bombs rained down on the civilian population, more than half a million people packed what they could carry and fled.

'The night of Monday October 30th 1995 was a black night in the entire history of the age-old City of Jaffna,' said the Reverend Father SJ Emmanuel, a Sri Lankan Tamil priest. 'Never has history witnessed such an exodus of fear and panic-stricken people screaming and squeezing themselves out of the narrow roads and lanes of Jaffna. Nearly half a million [people] in and around the town were literally on the roads in pouring rain, inching their way out of the densely populated town into the sparsely populated and ill-equipped suburban villages of the southern peninsula. For each of these 500,000 it was a flight for survival.'

The only exit from Jaffna to the south was over the tiny Navatkuli Bridge, which Para's mother had crossed on the way to the hospital to deliver her son. 'The number of civilians fleeing from the threat of Sri Lanka Army atrocities during that fateful night of October 30 reached an unbelievable three hundred thousand people in flight,' Father Emmanuel observed. He likened this many people rushing to cross this bridge with their belongings to the biblical camel attempting to go through the eye of a needle.

'The monsoon rains beating hard on the faces of weeping mothers and hungry children washed away the sweat and tears,' he continued. 'They were all drenched, not so much by the night rains but in the sorrows and pains of leaving their houses in the much-loved citadel of Jaffna. Most of them had to leave behind their treasured houses, furniture, gardens and produce not once, not twice but even thrice, before they undertook this ultimate flight to survive. There was a sorrowful silence enveloping the slow and reluctantly moving crowds. Whenever they spoke, each had a more sorrowful story to tell the other.'

The rush for survival was slowed down 'only by heavy hearts, massive crowding and bad roads,' he said. 'This panic- and fear-stricken population evacuating the peninsula was forced further to slow down as it approached the six-feet-narrow neck of the town—the Navatkuli Bridge. Here they were literally trying to inch their way out of the danger zone. True, they were moving out of a dangerous zone, but their destiny was still unknown and undecided.

'They had no choice between life and death,' Father Emmanuel said. 'For survival, they said, "Let us move out, as quickly as possible and with the maximum that we could carry with our hands, or on a cycle, or in a shared tractor or kerosene van." ... Once they passed the Navatkuli Bridge, the biggest question of survival was, "Where are we to seek shelter?" While standing for hours in the rains in that long queue towards some unknown destiny in the Thenmaradchchy and Vadamaradchi areas, babies cried for food and drink, some vehicles impatiently tooted their horns while all the others were sunk deep in their silence of sadness.'

Father Emmanuel described the desperate scenes: 'Either about fifteen people of all ages moving in a single row, or six or seven bicycles or kerosene-powered motorcycles, each loaded with at least two bags of personal belongings on the carrier, filled the narrow road. An elderly mother or father or baby was seated on the bar of a cycle either ridden or pushed by a younger son or daughter.

'Yet another scene was kerosene-oil-powered tractors with trailers loaded with people as well as a variety of things—mats, pillows, kerosene oil lamps, cooking utensils, domestic pets and some food stuff.

'A third pattern was that of a few well-to-do and the aged—an old Austin [A]40 car running on kerosene oil ... packed with one or two families, their belongings loaded into an open dicky and on the hood carrier. In between these modes of transport walked the majority poor with their half-naked little ones, most of them carrying at least one plastic bag of belongings—their goats and cows meekly following them.'

But even this inching in the rain ground to a halt when a heavily loaded lorry or tractor turned off the track, or one of its tyres went flat. 'Between 5 p.m. on Monday and 5 a.m. on Tuesday, three babies had died through the stampede and a pregnant mother gave birth on the road,' he said. 'Hundreds of the aged who crossed the bridge that night did not survive for long ... There was not a single good hospital outside Jaffna town to cater to the thousands who suffered.

'The pathetic exodus of people carried the inhuman marks of cruelty inflicted over a long time by many of the anti-Tamil measures taken by successive Sinhala governments, especially by the present one,' Father Emmanuel pointed out. 'The inhuman economic embargo enforced by the government on the Tamil people reduced them to primitive forms of life. The embargo on fuel and closure of the peninsula to outside vehicles made all petrol-fuelled vehicles disappear out of Jaffna. Only kerosene-fuelled motorcycles and old cars were available for transport.'

Those who made it across the bridge to the safer side went directly to the houses of relatives or friends. '… to each house in Thenmaradchchy and Vadamaradchi came not just one relative or friend … but several hundreds were knocking on their doors for help,' he said. 'Hence almost every house in Thenmaradchchy was flooded with friends—guests without prior notice—and had to host at least five to six families of instant refugees.'

Para remembers the massive displacement and the effect on his own village.

'There were just thousands and thousands of frightened people moving down from Jaffna to escape the bombs,' he says. 'Most people had nowhere to stay; many came to our village and made small shelters from bits of plastic. They were living all around the village, outside our small house, all around the pond, under the trees—just everywhere.'

Para's family didn't have much to share, but they managed to give them clean drinking water and some biscuits.

'People also settled in churches and temples, then the schools were all closed so people could stay in them. Everyone who came to our area had had to leave their own vegetable gardens and there was now no room for cultivation, so there was an extreme shortage of food. Luckily some volunteer organisations did manage to bring in some food for the refugees.'

In Colombo, Para's father and brother were also having a difficult time because every Tamil was suspected of being a Tamil Tiger, and they were constantly being dragged in for questioning and detained in police stations. 'Often, they never came out,' Para says. 'Sometimes Tamils were not allowed to use public transport, and they had to undergo endless security checks. Back home, there were so many people trying to get jobs that my mum could not find any work, so we usually didn't have any money at all—not a single rupee.'

Those displaced people without friends or relatives in the region could shelter in public places. However, Father Emmanuel said, 'the poorest of the poor were still left outside on the roadside, under trees, in old and dilapidated shelters at bus stops and in railway stations, unused for almost a decade.'

As if the inclement weather, the dewy nights, the food shortages, and problems of sanitation, shelter and medical care weren't enough, there were no organisational structures to meet such sudden and heavy demand.

'But with willing co-operation from all sides, the impossible ceased to be so,' Father Emmanuel said, crediting the LTTE for setting up help within two days of the exodus through the Tamil Rehabilitation Organisation, with the assistance of government agents, non-governmental and religious organisations. A network of services would cater to the minimum needs of such a massive population—'*cadjan*[2] shelters to protect the people from the rains, temporary toilet ditches to preserve sanitation, distribution of clothes, mats and sheets to stand the colder nights of November and dry rations or cooked food at least once a day kept the population alive.'

Despite their best efforts to survive, the refugees from Jaffna faced huge problems when government aid was halted.

---

2 Temporary shelters made from tarpaulins.

The displacement

Father Emmanuel reported that, 'The growing restrictions imposed by the government on the flow of food, medicine and other essential items for life, the restrictions of the NGOs in not allowing them to get their means of communication, the restrictions on the media and prohibition of journalists to the north, and continued aerial attacks even on the displaced population were all causing the slow death of the Tamil population as exiles even within their own homeland.'

Since the schools were all closed, Para started teaching. 'Every day around one hundred children aged from five to sixteen would come to our house,' he says, 'and I would teach them, class by class. Before I began each class I would ask the students if they had showered and brushed their teeth that day. We might have been poor, but we could still be clean! Everyone washed by the pond, and broke a twig off a special bush for cleaning their teeth.

'No one had pencils or paper to write on, so I used the door of our house as a notebook and a blackboard. This meant it was difficult when Mum or Grandma wanted to go in or out of the house! Later, some of the parents managed to find some smooth timber, and they painted it black so then I had a proper blackboard and we hung it on the wall so it didn't open and close with the door, which made life easier for everyone.'

Para taught reading, writing, Tamil, maths and science to children from Grades 1 to 5; each age group went for one hour each day, four or five days each week. Around thirty to forty children in each class sat on the ground outside his house. 'When it was dark, we would hang a hurricane lamp off a stick,' he says. 'No one had any money, but the refugees were given some food each month by the government because of being displaced, so they would pay me for their lessons in rice, flour, chilli and coconuts. This way our family had enough to eat.'

Soon after these dreadful events, Father Emmanuel observed: 'The deaths and destruction in the north-east of Sri Lanka through so many military operations—Leap Forward, Thunder Strike, Hand Shake and Riviresa, just to mention a few within a short period of three months in the tiny peninsula—may remain hidden or covered up for many years, but truth will emerge sooner than later. And hopefully there will be still time for repentance and reconciliation.'

He pointed out that, 'Already three months have elapsed since the alien Sinhala Military occupied Jaffna and chased out the indigenous population. The world has neither known the whole truth of this exodus and massive suffering, nor has any government condemned the actions of the Sri Lanka Government for its inhuman military action. Thus, the world which is quick to condemn the counter violence of a desperate people but reluctant, if not sinfully silent, to condemn state terror or to search out and treat the underlying cause of violence, will one day wake up to this reality and answer its own conscience.'

Para hoped this latest massive offensive against the Tamils and the ensuing displacement would be an end to the disruption.

'I was only sixteen, so I was still young enough to be optimistic,' he says. 'Life was bearable. I enjoyed teaching the children, we all had just enough food to survive—although everyone was always hungry. We were all living very closely together, many people just packed in under plastic sheets, but we were alive, and we were essentially okay. I wanted to go back to school to study, but for now I just hoped that everything would work out. I thought it would.

'I could not have been more wrong.'

6

THE RUNNING

The war was becoming dangerously close. No one was spared, and people from Para's village had already suffered extensively in a previous bombing raid.

The army was moving relentlessly through the area, intent on taking over the district of Jaffna. To avoid more civilian casualties, the LTTE instructed everyone to move southwards, into the LTTE-controlled Vanni area of the Kilinochchi District. Some Jaffna city Tamils who had been forced from their homes a few weeks beforehand decided to risk death and return to their homes in the city, but most believed safety lay south, so another huge displacement began. This time, Para and his family were part of it.

By now they knew the terror of war only too well, but it was still difficult to decide to leave. Everything they had was in that village—their land on which they grew their vegetables, the coconut trees they had planted and tended for generations, the pond that supplied them with fish and water for the gardens, and their houses that they had built with their own hands.

The running

And if they did leave, they did not know if they could ever return—indeed, many displaced families in other areas who tried to return found their land had been taken over by the Sri Lankan government and new families had moved into their homes and onto their farms. But the decision to go or to stay was made for them when fighting between the Sri Lanka Army and the LTTE intensified, and shells and mortars started raining down.

'My dad had heard the news of this next displacement,' Para says, 'and he was so worried about us that he travelled all the way from Colombo back to our village to help us to move quickly, ahead of the big rush. It was a real problem to get away from the area because there was only one land route—across Elephant Pass—but this was dominated by a big Sri Lanka Army base, and they were shelling people who tried to leave. So we knew we had to go by sea.

'Thousands and thousands of people were moving to Kilali because they all thought the only possibility was to try to get on a boat there. Dad heard that some people were fleeing across the Jaffna Lagoon hidden in fishing boats, but soldiers from the Sri Lanka Army camp at Pooneryn were watching the sea and shooting at anyone they thought was trying to escape.'

They had to decide very quickly what to do.

'Dad thought the only possibility was for us to walk to another village—Maravanpulavu—and to find someone to take us across in their fishing boat,' Para says. 'We quickly grabbed everything we could carry and moved out of our village, joining with absolutely thousands of other people. It felt like millions of us. My sister was just thirteen, and we had Grandma and Tiger, of course, so we had to be careful not to lose them in the crush. We walked and walked and walked—it was so far, we seemed to walk slowly and forever, but Grandma never complained.

'I carried a bag containing milk powder, sugar, candles and matches and a few tea bags. We could not bring cooking pots or kitchen equipment. We each brought one change of clothes, and grandma and mum each had a spare sari. That was all. Everything else we possessed, we left behind. We never went back.

'Finally, we reached Maravanpulavu and met a fisherman, who told us it would be dangerous for us all if the Sri Lanka Army soldiers saw us. But we had no better plan, so we all went to his house and waited until darkness fell, then we crept to the beach.'

The fishing boat was tiny, so they could only bring small bags with important documents and one set of clothes each.

'I carried Grandma across the water to the boat and put her in, then helped my mum and sister,' Para recounts. 'We were all told to hide under the nets, so if any soldiers shone their spotlights at the boat they would think it was just an ordinary fishing boat and leave us alone. Then I hurried back for Tiger, but the fisherman told me it was not possible to bring the dog—if he barked, the soldiers would know there were people on the boat and would kill us all.

'I couldn't believe we had to leave our loyal dog, but I knew the fisherman was right. I hugged Tiger one last time and told him to stay on the beach, then I waded back to the boat, climbed in and hid under the nets with my family.

'We set sail and I could hear splashing—it was Tiger swimming alongside the boat, whining. We were all crying. After some time we no longer heard him, and I think he must have swum back to the shore. I felt wretched. I had betrayed a loyal best friend. My heart ached—I had not even been able to say goodbye. I am so sorry, Tiger.

'I had grown up knowing war. Now I felt that war knew me—it knew how to hurt.'

* * *

For more than two hours they sailed silently across the calm water, barely daring to breathe, until they reached the Pooneryn Bridge. The army knew about the narrow channel there and the soldiers stationed themselves on the bridge, weaving their massive spotlights from side to side, checking all the fishing boats passing below. Para and his family could only lie as still as possible beneath the nets, hearts thumping, resisting all temptation to move or to peer out.

Para grasped his grandmother's trembling hand and they prayed together silently, aware that detection would mean instant death.

'Grandma was very frightened, more for us than for herself, and I could feel her little hand shaking in mine,' Para says. 'But I was too sad about Tiger to feel anything.'

Finally, they passed under the bridge and reached the Vanni side at about 3 a.m. An LTTE patrol boat found them and took them to the shore, where they were told to line up along the beach for checking. They paid the fisherman because he had to be back before sunrise, and Para asked him to look out for Tiger when he returned.

'He put his hand on my shoulder and promised me he would search for Tiger and care for him,' Para recalls. 'Then he pushed out his boat, hopped on board and quietly sailed away into the darkness. I prayed he would be safe, and that he would find Tiger and keep him for when I returned.

'We were all devastated when we heard a few months later that the Sri Lanka Army had killed the kind fisherman as he sailed back that morning. The fishermen were allowed to be in the ocean. Fishing was their livelihood. They should have been safe, but too often the soldiers just shot them as if for sport, leaving their families destitute.'

On the shore, Para's father told the LTTE soldiers that they wanted to go to his wife's second brother's house in Kiranchi.

'Uncle Kunam didn't know we were coming and there were no phones, so we had no way of telling him,' Para says. 'But we were told to climb into an old truck with other people who had fled our area, and we set off in the dark along very bumpy, broken roads, full of huge potholes and craters. Everything was damaged by the war, so it took ages to drive slowly through the villages, and people were dropped off one by one or in small family groups.

'Finally, we arrived at my uncle's house. Although he was very surprised to see us, he was very kind and overjoyed to know we were safe, especially my mum—his sister—and of course, Grandma—his mum. He had a tiny house, like ours had been, but we all squeezed in anyway, and he made us welcome. Although they had very little because the government had stopped allowing supplies into the Vanni area, they shared everything, and Uncle even found some clothes for us. There was no kerosene for lanterns, so at night we would make a small fire from sticks and wood, and sitting around it we would talk about the latest news from the war and wonder what was going to happen next.'

In the Vanni area, the Sri Lankan government limited supplies of many things. 'Milk powder, kerosene, candles, matchboxes were allowed in very limited quantities and those were very expensive,' Para says. 'There was no electricity, and kerosene for lamps was too expensive, so it was hard to study at night—I had to study in the daytime, like other Tamil children.'

Para remembers how severely his kind Uncle Kunam was affected by the war. Two of his six children—Para's cousins Gowsala, aged thirty-four, and Kunesh, aged nineteen—were killed in a Sri Lanka Army airstrike while they were sheltering in a bunker. Gowsala had a baby who survived. Kunam's third son Kannan lost his wife in another shell attack, leaving Kannan with four children to care for.

'Such a tragedy,' Para says, 'but the greater tragedy was that this was happening to innocent families everywhere.'

At first there was barely any food and life was extremely difficult for everyone, but after a few weeks the United Nations High Commission for Refugees (UNHCR) managed to organise a food convoy into the Vanni area and limited amounts of flour, rice, sugar and kerosene became available. Many thousands more people had arrived by now, and once again everyone began to organise themselves, and settle in. It was a tight squeeze in his uncle's house, so Para's father decided to make a temporary home from mud and coconut leaves.

They tried to return to a more normal life.

'We realised we would be here for some time, maybe years, so it was time to think about our education,' Para says. 'Uncle Kunam lived in a village that didn't have a high school, so Dad decided I should go to stay with my mother's youngest brother, Uncle Ganesh, in a village called Skandapuram, about fifty kilometres away. He then managed to find an old bicycle so we could get there.

'I was very sad to leave my family, and especially Grandma, but we all knew I had to get back to school and this was the only option. Mum told me that Uncle Ganesh was very, very poor—even poorer than us? I couldn't imagine it!—so I would have to help him a lot, as well as concentrate and work hard at school. Grandma held me very tightly and told me to study hard and to be a good boy, then she pressed some roti into my hand for us to eat on the journey, and we set off.

'The jungle came right up to the edge of the road, which was full of huge potholes. Some were natural, others had been made by bombs. When it rained, they filled with water and the road was slippery and even more dangerous. We had to keep an eye open for unexploded shells and travel carefully—not that two people sharing an old bicycle can go very fast!'

It took all day to reach Uncle Ganesh's home, and Para and his father were both exhausted from the difficult journey.

'My uncle was very pleased to see us. He didn't have a farm, but he knew about the land and he had a small garden where he grew corn and tapioca. Most days, we ate tapioca—only tapioca. Uncle didn't have a well but he lived near to the pond, so to get clean water we had to dig a hole, let the water level rise in it, scoop out the water from the bottom, then boil the water before we could drink it. I quickly realised that although we had not had much, Uncle Ganesh had next to nothing.

'During a very heavy rainy season we had absolutely no food to eat, and not even one rupee, so Uncle asked me to earn some money working for his friend in the forests. The torrential rain poured down endlessly, but we worked non-stop all day from dawn to dusk regardless, and even found some forest fruits to eat. I must have done well, because after that day the friend asked me to continue working there, so I helped him every weekend and in the school holidays. My hands became very hard and scratched and when the rain was heavy I tried to keep my head dry by wearing a plastic shopping bag on it. I must have looked terrible in my plastic "hat", old vest and torn sarong.

'My new school friends soon realised that I was working in the forest,' Para says. 'They did not laugh at me, though; instead, they made a roster among themselves and brought food to me. I could not have survived without them.

'As well, I became very close to my thirteen-year old-cousin, Kuddi. If we didn't have any food for breakfast he would go and find a coconut, and break it into small pieces. He often tried to give me his portion but I always told him to eat his own share. I was terribly sad to hear that near the end of the war, a Sri Lanka Army shell landed on the bunker where he was sheltering with his brother Jana, his brother's wife and their small baby. Kuddi and the baby died instantly; Jana survived, but his wife lost one leg, one hand and an eye.'

Para regrets that he hardly ever managed to visit his mother's oldest brother—his first Uncle Sothy—because he lived farther away at Mallavi and the roads were so bad that it was impossible to even ride a bicycle there. The war also affected him badly, as his younger son Sabesh was killed.

'I really loved those three uncles. They were so poor, but they always shared what little they had, and they were endlessly kind.'

Para soon adapted to life with his Uncle Ganesh and his cousins, and he managed to settle in quickly to his new school, Akkarayankulam Maha Vidyalayam.

However, Para still had a long journey around a large lake each day, so he had to get up very early to complete all his chores and arrive on time. Punctuality at the school was extremely important, and students who arrived late were routinely hit across the hands with sticks. As if this wasn't enough, Para soon realised that if he wanted to obtain grades that would be good enough for university he would also have to study each morning at the private school, which was about three kilometres in the other direction.

'I could not afford the fees at the private school but I really wanted to attend, so I made myself brave and I went there to ask for free lessons,' he says. 'The receptionist said it was not possible, but then I happened to see a teacher called Kanakalingam from my other school who was also working there. I waited outside his classroom and when he came out I told him that I wanted to study but I couldn't afford to pay. He was very kind, and told me I could study in his class, and that I should ask all the other teachers for free lessons. So, I did, and they all helped me—Kanakalingam, Thirupathy, Mahendran and Sris. I am so grateful to them.

The running

'From then, my days were crazy busy. I would waken very early, wash and dress, do whatever chores my uncle wanted, then I would rush out through the door and run to the private school, study there, then straight after classes finished at 8.30 a.m. I would run all the way to the government school.'

The problem was that lessons at the private school finished only half an hour before lessons at the government school commenced, so Para was almost certain to be late every day. His fellow students managed because they could travel easily between the schools on their bicycles, but Para had to run. Every day, he was caught by the principal and beaten on his hands. Para did not like to say that he had been attending classes at the private school, so he accepted the beating as a part of his day.

Two girls—Saila and Komala—lived between Para's uncle's house and the private school. They cycled to the gate of their house and had great fun watching Para run from home to the private school and then on to the government school.

'My clothes were worn and tattered and they would ride their bicycles to the end of the road and laugh: "Look, there he goes, running with his torn pants hanging down." I was ashamed and embarrassed but there was nothing I could do except run.

'Then one day Komala called to me: "Hey, we have laughed at you enough—can we help you instead?" and they offered me one of their bicycles.

'In our culture, it was not allowed for me to speak to the girls in public, so we had to be careful. We made a plan for the girls to meet me halfway to the private school and to lend me one of their bicycles. I could then ride this to the private school, complete the early-morning lessons there, then ride on to the other school, arriving in time for classes and avoiding the beating. The girls would then share the other bike. In the afternoon, I could ride back almost to their house, and then leave the bike in the bushes and run the last part of the way to my uncle's.'

Para's life changed—he was no longer late every day, he did not have to run with his bag and books, but just cycle easily along with the other students. It meant a lot to be able to ride with the others and not to be the poor boy, always late and always running.

'I would love to thank Saila and Komala for this small act of kindness that made the world of difference to me. There was a downside, of course—there always is! Sometimes one of the girls would be sick or just decide to miss school, so then there was no bicycle ... on those days I was terribly late for both schools, and then I would really feel the bite of the stick on my hands!'

As well as lending Para a bike, the girls started to prepare food for his lunches.

'In the morning before school there was no time for eating—and there was never any food anyway—so when the teachers banged the saucepans at 11 a.m., calling the very poor students to go to the dining room for the rice porridge they called *kanchi*, I was never too proud to go along with them. I would turn up with my metal spoon and bowl and devour the *kanchi* hungrily. Most of the other students would wait until lunchtime and eat the food their mothers had prepared.

'After a few weeks, Saila and Komala started bringing extra food for me, and then some of the other students would take me with them to the canteen and buy me food. I always hoped that one day I would be able to repay them, or at least to thank them for taking me under their wings.'

The girls did Para another good turn. They talked about him to their friend, the daughter of the school principal, and told her that they loaned him their bike. This girl must have told her father what was happening because one day—a day when Para had arrived late because the bike had not been available—the principal asked him where he had been.

'I just told him that I had slept in, and that was why I was late. He made me stand on one side while he caned all the other late arrivals, then he asked me again. This time I told him the truth and after that he never caned me again, even on days when the arrangement with the bike fell through and I had to run, and I arrived long after the first bell.'

7

EDUCATION AND ENTERPRISE

Against the backdrop of civil war, with all the fighting and the dangers posed by the Sri Lanka Army, the security forces and the LTTE, you might think that all normal life ceased and everything fell into chaos. But this was not the case. Everyone knew how important it was to acquire a good education and get high grades, so they all continued studying.

But although they were happy enough and studied hard, Para recalls the underlying tension.

'Almost every day the cadres from the Tamil Tigers would approach us,' he says. 'They had several methods of contacting us; most mornings they would drive around the district playing Tamil songs very loudly on a speaker, interspersed with messages and invitations for us to join them. So, from the very start of every day we were thinking about the Tigers and the war, and the need for us to join them in the fight for independence. Then, when we were cycling to school, they would leave their bicycles by the side of the road and wave us down as we passed. At first, they would just ask us our names, and then questions about our homes and families. They soon became familiar with everyone's situation.

'I was different from the others because, until I borrowed Komala's bike, I was always running or walking quickly, and they could see I just didn't have the time to stop.'

However, one Tiger did stop Para. Kannan oversaw the political wing in the Skandapuram area. He had noticed the dishevelled, shoeless teenager racing between the schools. One day he called Para from across the road and asked why he was always running, and where he had left his shoes.

'I told him I was living with my uncle because we had been displaced from our home village, and that we were all extremely poor,' Para says. 'He invited me to go with him to the LTTE camp, where he promised to find me some shoes. I told my uncle that night; he said it was better that I refused because he did not want me to end up joining the LTTE—"Imagine me trying to explain that to your mum!". But I couldn't see any harm in going to the camp, and I was quite curious to see what happened there, so the next day I told Kannan I would go with him, and he gave me some plastic sandals. Later, he gave me an old pair of proper shoes. It all helped me to get to school on time.'

Para saw Kannan regularly for the next few weeks, as the LTTE soldier was also stopping other students as they travelled to school.

'The soldiers would ask the students if they would like to join them,' Para says. 'Sometimes a young person may have simply had an argument with their parents before leaving for school, and for that reason they might agree to go to the camp, where they would be given a uniform and become a part of the LTTE. The parents would go to the camp and cry, and try to get their son or daughter back, but once they had signed up, that was it. Later, the students would discover just what they had got themselves into, but it was too late by then. They could never leave. I was lucky because Kannan never asked me to sign up—I think he must have seen that my uncle really needed me.'

Para had another interaction with the LTTE.

'In the jungle were many huge trees,' he says. 'The LTTE was extremely careful about protecting the forests, and people were prohibited from taking the trees. But sometimes the only way my uncle could make any money was by felling a tree and selling the timber to a local man with a timber mill. It was dangerous to do this because who knew what the Tigers would do if they caught us? But we had to do it anyway, or starve.

'One day, during a monsoonal downpour, we managed to get our cart deep into the jungle and we cut just one tree and cleaned it and took it to the mill. We didn't like to steal a tree, but really there was no alternative. We weren't caught, probably because it was raining so heavily that no one was around. We sold the timber and that meant we could eat for a week or so, and we kept the thin branches and leaves for repairing Uncle's house.

'A few weeks later we had run out of food again—we had no food for breakfast or lunch, just some tea with a twist of sugar if we were lucky. So we went back into the jungle. But this time it was not raining. We should have been more careful, but we were desperate. After a little while, we had found the tree we wanted and we were chopping at it with the axe when we heard twigs breaking and boots running and realised we were surrounded.

'"Come out now or we'll shoot you!" they shouted, so we walked out of the jungle and were immediately arrested by LTTE soldiers. They took us to their camp and they were furious with us. We felt ashamed, but we told them we had no other way of making an income for the family. They realised how poor we were, so decided to punish Uncle by making him stay at the camp for a week, cleaning and cooking for the soldiers.

'They were wondering what to do with me when Kannan arrived.

'"What are you doing here?" he asked me. I told him, hoping he could help me.

'"Rules are rules," he replied. By now I was scared because I knew we had committed a crime.

'Then he just said, "Oh go home, and study hard."

'I was very grateful. And no, I never cut another tree again, and yes, I really did study hard! But I should have known that Kannan would not forget me.'

When the exams came around the Tamil students were faced with another problem—the government allocated quotas for further education in each district, depending on ethnicity. This meant that to secure a place at university all Tamil students had to do particularly well and score in the first ten.

'I managed to come eighteenth in the district, with a score that I thought was reasonable—220 marks. But I may as well have come last, because eighteenth was certainly not good enough, no matter what I thought. Sinhalese students scoring much lower marks were given university places. It was so unfair, but there was nothing I could do.'

Except try again—the following year Para worked even harder, racing to complete his chores, to get to the private lessons and the school lessons, to help his uncles, to visit his mother, little sister and grandmother back in Kiranchi, and earn money selling coconuts and bananas.

The borrowed bicycle came in handy for travelling to Kiranchi. It was a long and difficult journey—around fifty kilometres—but Para liked to check on his mother, grandmother and Pugalini since his father had returned to Colombo to stay with Panneer.

While Uncle Ganesh did not have his own land, he did have unlimited access to bananas, so the two of them conceived an idea for making a few rupees.

'A few rupees can be the difference between eating or going without,' Para says. 'We thought about what we had, and what we could sell, and my uncle came up with the idea for me to buy bananas from the local farmers and take them on my bicycle to the next town, where my mum was living with my grandma and younger sister—and where bananas did not grow—so we could sell them for a little more than we had paid to buy them.'

So, each weekend, Para would tie heavy bunches of bananas to his bicycle frame and make the journey to Kiranchi. After a while he found other people were involved in the same business of transporting bananas, so they joined up and rode through the jungle together.

'The roads were terrible, with massive potholes in the dirt road from shelling, and large rocks and trees strewn across the roads all causing great problems as we rode, trying to stop the bananas from banging against the bicycles and bruising. Punctures happened all the time, and often one of us would have to just push his bicycle nearly the whole way, with the flat tyres dragging over the rough ground. Of course, we were always hungry, but we kept going because there was no alternative—we were all trying to earn extra rupees. When there was no moon and it became too dark to see, we had to listen out for each other and just try to stay on the road and not stray into the jungle.'

It was scary—and they could hear wild animals in the jungle—but they continued this weekly pilgrimage.

'Then one week after we had delivered our bananas I had a brilliant idea—our village had bananas but no coconuts, while the village where Mum lived had coconuts … I saw a wonderful business opportunity. All Tamils love coconuts— we depend on them for cooking, for the milk they contain, for the hemp we can scrape off them … it seemed a good idea for me to take them back to my uncle's village and sell them.'

Within a few weeks, Para and his new friends had a great system—loaded with bananas they cycled their perilous way to Kiranchi, then the next day, loaded with coconuts, they made their way back. Coconuts were as awkward to carry as bananas, but at least they did not bruise. With bags crammed full of coconuts hanging at the front and the back of their bicycles, the boys each managed to carry around 100 coconuts on every trip. Para sometimes wonders what Australia's occupational health and safety inspectors would make of those teenagers struggling with overladen, ancient bicycles.

Falling off a bicycle or stepping on unexploded shells, although constant hazards, were the least of their concerns.

'We heard a lot of crashing in the undergrowth, and we were frightened pretty much all the time. Big cats inhabit the jungle—the wild ones with four legs as well as the two-legged ones with guns and grenades!—and we were always wary of them. But we were not as frightened of them as of the other mighty kings of the jungle—elephants. Often we would see family groups close by and we were always respectful and kept as much distance as we could manage.'

The destruction of the jungle was yet one more thing the Sri Lankan civil war was responsible for, so the wild animals found their world was shrinking. These elephants were truly wild—it was, after all, their jungle—but on the whole, they kept themselves as far away from humans as possible.

Para could not help admiring them as they strolled along, huge and patient, their eyes sad and questioning. 'They had no fight with us, as long as we respected their right to move freely ahead of us—or behind, or alongside, or anywhere they chose!'

However, after a few weeks they became aware of another elephant—a massive bull that was separate from the herd. Para didn't know much about elephant ecology, but it seemed that this one was a loner—he wandered through the jungle bellowing and knocking down trees.

'One evening as we pushed, rode or dragged our bicycles, laden with bananas, he came rushing towards us,' Para remembers. 'You can't imagine our fear—he was truly gigantic, and very angry. The leaders of the group yelled, "Quickly, throw down your bananas and run!" so we all did just that, and somehow everyone escaped. But of course, we had no bananas to sell when we arrived in Kiranchi, and no one wanted to hear our excuses.'

The next week, after the boys had loaded up with bananas ready for the perilous trek, one of them made a lantern from coconut oil and they felt brave and confident because someone had read somewhere that elephants are frightened of fire. They approached the spot where they knew the big bull elephant would be waiting like a highwayman—elephants are so clever that he would have known this was an easy way to score some delicious bananas.

'We lit the lamp, and stayed close, swinging the lamp in the hope the elephant would be too scared to approach. Looking back, it's quite sad—fourteen children (we thought we were brave men but really, we were just hungry boys needing to get home safely to do our homework) trying to outwit an old bull elephant with a tin can burning coconut oil, the flame from a thick wick supported above the oil by a stick.

'Of course, as soon as he caught our scent he came charging through the bushes, heading straight for us. "Throw down your bananas and run!" came the call. We immediately scattered, bananas flying everywhere, but I did the opposite—I jumped on my bike behind the bananas and pedalled as fast as I could, avoiding the elephant and reaching the safety of the trees on the other side. The boy with the lantern had to jump off his bike and narrowly escaped the elephant, who threw himself at the lantern and flattened the bike.

'I will never forget seeing that massive creature bearing down on the flimsy bicycle, boys fleeing in every direction, the bananas cascading across the road, the terrible roar of the angry elephant and the frightened shouts of the boys.'

They managed to regroup a few minutes later—all safe, but only Para had managed to keep his bananas; the others were either squashed or being devoured by the old bull elephant.

'I don't know what made me hang onto my bananas—I think I was so tired from the long, hard cycling that I could not bear to lose them, and I knew my family needed every rupee.'

Para still dreams about that dark night, and the huge elephant racing towards them.

'I feel the ground shaking and I hear the shouts and the crashing and then the crunch of the bicycle, flattened by the elephant's knees. And I wonder if he is still there in the jungle, waiting for boys and bananas. The boy with the lantern was not a close friend—we lost touch and I sometimes wonder what happened to him. It was a good idea to try waving a lantern, it's a shame it didn't work. Never mind, *nanri*—thanks—to him for trying.'

They all struggled on, and Para started to save a few rupees from this fledgling business, squeezed in between the chores for his uncle, visits to his mother, lessons at school, extra tutorials and examinations.

The year passed in a blur, and the exams came around so quickly that he was almost taken by surprise.

But this time he was better prepared, and he knew that he was answering the questions well. When he received the letter telling him he had come third in the district, he knew that he was going to be able to fulfil his dream of attending university.

Para was eligible to apply to either University of Peradeniya at Kandy in the middle of the country, or University of Jaffna in the north. It was such a great feeling—for once in his life, it seemed he had a choice.

But the feeling was short-lived because, actually, there was no choice. With Sri Lankan government forces still fighting the LTTE, it was just about impossible for civilians to travel—the main road from the Vanni region to the centre of the country was always under attack, there were hundreds of checkpoints and the journey was perilous.

'So really, I had to stay in the north, and I applied to study at Jaffna University. I was happy and proud to be going there—the first person in my family to manage such a thing.'

Towards the end of 2000, Para was officially offered a place to study for a Bachelor of Arts degree in economics at University of Jaffna.

'I feel I owe part of my success in the exams to Saila and Komala,' he says. 'Thanks to them—and many other friends whose names I can't mention because they are still living in Sri Lanka—I made it to all the classes and tutorials, I stopped being late to school and avoided the cane. Because of them, the principal understood that I was not the lazy boy he first suspected. And they even made sure I had good food so I could concentrate on the lessons more than my empty stomach. They probably don't even remember lending me their bicycle, but I will never forget it.'

Para can never thank Komala now. When he recently came across her brother on social media and asked him to pass a message to her, he learned that she was yet another innocent victim of the war—killed in a bombardment in 2002.

THE ROAD TO UNIVERSITY

In late October 2000, the students living in the Vanni area who had been successful in their Advanced Level examinations received letters from the University Grants Commission telling them to gather in the closest town of Vavuniya, ready for their next big adventure—University of Jaffna.

Para was as excited as the rest of the young men. And all around the world, new batches of students were making their way to their universities. But this was a country embroiled in a civil war so it was not just a case of driving, or boarding a train or a bus, to reach their destination. Jaffna was less than 200 kilometres from Vavuniya, yet almost ten days would pass by the time the new students finally arrived in the university town.

Leaving his family, especially his mother and grandmother, was hard.

'Of course, they were delighted and proud, but they really worried about the threats and dangers,' he says. 'We all knew people who had been maimed, kidnapped and killed, young girls and men who had been raped and murdered by soldiers from the Sri Lanka Army, and young people virtually kidnapped by the LTTE and forced to fight. So many families were devastated by this war. But we simply had to go on and live as normally as we could. It was sometimes too hard to bear the weight of these terrible events but, on the whole, we managed.'

Then it was time to visit Uncle Ganesh, Cousin Kuddi and their family. Para cycled for two hours through the muddy jungle tracks, carefully looking out for the big bull elephant.

'That was one creature I did not want to see again,' he says. 'But I'm sad to know he'll almost certainly be dead by now. At the end of the war the fighting was so intense that all the forest and jungle was smashed by bombs and vehicles. Elephants, wild cats, monkeys—everything was destroyed. Any animals that survived the shelling would have died because their habitats had been demolished. I wish I had known that would be the last time, ever, that I would be riding along the track—but if I knew then what the future held for me, I may have been tempted to stay and not even think about university.'

Para had to shave before leaving his uncle's house, because all new students had to observe various customs imposed by the seniors.

'It was part of the "ragging" system—we had to have clean skin, so I shaved,' he says. 'Also, we were not allowed to wear watches, belts or proper shoes. That was easy for me, as I only possessed plastic sandals. My cousin Kuddi watched me shave and prepare for university life, and I explained to him that after three months the seniors would hold a party for the new students, after which we were allowed to grow moustaches and dress normally. It was like an induction, and showed respect to the seniors.

'I will always remember that last time spent explaining things to Kuddi. He had welcomed me into the family, and was like a little brother to me. He was sad to be saying goodbye, but he cheered up when I gave him my bicycle. Again, I wonder if I would have managed to leave him if I had known that he was also going to be killed.'

Para had already received a travel pass from the LTTE to enable him to leave the area—it had been granted quickly, along with a message for all the students to work hard and well—so it was time to meet up with his friends and some seniors from the University of Jaffna, who came to guide the new students. Uncle Ganesh walked with Para to the temple, where they had all arranged to meet, then together the excited boys made their way to the bus stop, everyone carrying just a small bag with some clothes.

The journey had begun.

'The bus was packed as usual; we boys all stood so the women and older people could sit,' Para says. 'There was not much talking because everyone feared spies—no one dared to criticise the government or talk about the war, so only a few people were speaking in quiet voices. The Vanni, where we came from, was in an LTTE-controlled area, so everything was rationed, or impossible to obtain, but in the army-controlled areas it was easy to buy anything—if you had the money. Sri Lanka is such a small country that it was hard to believe there could be such a difference between two adjoining areas, but they were worlds apart.

'Many people on the bus were carrying empty two- and five-litre cans because they could only get kerosene from the shops in Vavuniya, and then only in small quantities. It was also hard to buy rice and many vegetables. I remember once Dad managed to bring some apples from Vavuniya for us. This was such a treat—they must have been imported from India or New Zealand, and there was no hope of getting anything as exotic from the shops in the Vanni area. My uncle sliced them very thinly and we each had a small piece. I can still remember the texture and taste.'

The journey should not have taken more than thirty to forty minutes, but the road was so bad that the bus had to creep around potholes, bomb craters and deep muddy puddles, swinging and sliding through the red dirt. The open sides and windows meant they were all soon covered in dust, and the trip ended up taking around four hours.

When the bus finally crawled into the town, the first thing Para noticed was how bright it was. 'It was evening and in the Vanni you would have been lucky to have seen just a few homes with a lamp glowing, as most people tried to make their kerosene last. But here there was electricity, and shops selling things we had only imagined. We had not realised how deprived people were who lived in the Vanni, or how the government kept Tamils in such poor conditions.'

It took around a week for the students to be issued with passes and tickets from the Government Agent's Office for the port of Trincomalee. Passes were essential in case of a round-up—young Tamils travelling without a pass were likely to be arrested and disappear without trace. Finally, everyone was organised and they left Vavuniya on buses, with each bus escorted by armed government soldiers in case of attack from LTTE soldiers.

'Civilians were always under threat from either LTTE soldiers or government soldiers,' Para says. 'We often felt crushed between the two armies.'

At last they reached Trincomalee and around 7 p.m. they all embarked on the ship that was to take them on the next stage of the journey. The *Spirit of Trinco* was operated by the International Committee of the Red Cross and transported sick people from Trincomalee to the hospital in Jaffna.

'We saw many patients loaded on and felt very sorry for them, having to make such a long journey by sea instead of going directly by road. The dock was very busy, and everywhere armed soldiers and sailors from the government forces were watching everyone, trying to be prepared in case of an attack from the LTTE. People were quite nervous, so it was a relief when the engines roared, the huge ropes were slipped off the bollards, and *Spirit of Trinco* slowly pulled away from the wharf. Immediately we headed out to open waters, away from the coastline in case the Sea Tigers, the sea wing of the LTTE, attacked.

'We were happy to be on the ship—at last we were making good progress—but it rocked and rolled so much that we were all terribly sick for the whole journey and extremely relieved when we sailed into Point Pedro, on the northernmost tip of the island, some sixteen hours later. From the port, we were taken into Jaffna town where the university staff met us to take us the final few kilometres to the university. We were completely exhausted, and so happy to be there.

It's lucky we all enjoyed our university years, as going home to visit relatives was just so difficult.'

Once in Jaffna, the students were photographed and each given emergency university ID while they organised the rest of their papers.

'It was essential to carry identity cards at all times,' Para says. 'We already had our Sri Lankan national cards, then after registering our addresses with the police we were given a university ID card and a special army ID. The cards would help us to explain our reasons for being in Jaffna, in case of a round-up or an arbitrary arrest.

'We were all Tamils, and the university was in a Sri Lanka Army-controlled area, so we were told to exercise extreme care and caution, to stay in a student hostel rather than independently with friends, to observe the curfews. There was so much advice and so many warnings that we wondered what we had come to. We thought university would be a place where we could study freely and enjoy our lives now that we had put the displacements and the examinations behind us. But we were Tamils—we should have known better.

'Anyway, nothing could dampen our enthusiasm, and we were excited to be in Jaffna. The war had meant that it was impossible for us to travel easily and, unless we had been displaced, most of us had not been out of our villages before, so it was a real experience to travel and to see Jaffna for the first time.'

The students were then taken to a large hall and told to find their names on the lists pasted to the walls. This would tell them which hostel they would be living in, after which they could slowly start to find their way around the university.

Senior students arrived to help the freshmen. Para searched the lists for his name but it did not appear on any of them. Soon, most of the students had worked out where they would be staying, and nearly all had left the hall.

'I was just beginning to get anxious when two much older students arrived. They were very friendly, confident and laughing.

'"Are you Para?" they asked. "Kannan told us about you—you're coming with us."

'I felt very young and quite intimidated by them, but next thing I was on the back of one of their motorbikes and we were zooming through the streets, past government soldiers and army vehicles. I had no idea where we were going or how they knew my name. But they seemed friendly and welcoming.

'We finally pulled up outside an ordinary looking house and we all went inside. "This is Para!" they called as we walked through the door.

'The first thing I saw was another student leaning over a table on which was lying a big automatic gun, all in pieces. My heart stopped. I quickly slammed the door shut. I was already sweating.

'What are you doing?' I hissed. 'The army are everywhere, what if they came in here and found you with a gun?'

'It's not a "gun" Para, it's an AK-47. Don't worry, relax, we know what we are doing.' They all found my terror quite funny, but really, I was truly frightened and I did not know how I had come to be with these students.

'They showed me where I would be sleeping, then said it was time to go out again. Back on the bike and off we went.

The road to university

Once again, I had no idea where we were heading. But then I saw crowds forming and soon realised we were in the middle of a huge demonstration. I had no idea what was going on.'

Para asked the driver what was happening.

'We are here to protest about the killing of Mylvaganam Nimalrajan,' he told Para.

'Who?'

'A senior Jaffna journalist who was shot by government sympathisers because he reported intimidation and election malpractice.'

Looking at the thousands of protesters, Para wondered what he was doing there.

'I had come to university, hoping for a quiet and safe life studying economics and then maybe getting a good teaching job with the government, which would enable me to finally look after my mum and uncles, so they would not have to creep into the jungle and steal trees, or take coconuts and bananas past rogue elephants, or pull roots from the ponds to make a meal. Those were my dreams and intentions that morning, but here I was now in the middle of a student demonstration that would surely end badly … I just prayed no one would see me, or recognise me.'

Then Para saw the photographers and the TV cameras.

'I only wanted to return to my room in the student house, because by then, I thought, the AK-47 would have been hidden safely and it would be a place of refuge,' he says.

It was a big and memorable day, so he was relieved when it ended with no violence and they all finally arrived back at the house and fell into bed, exhausted.

But just as he was slipping off to sleep, he heard quiet

whispers, gentle bumps and scrapes as if furniture was being moved. He also thought he heard low moaning.

Oh no. Now what?

'I went quietly through to the main room and saw a man lying on the floor, my housemates kneeling around him.

'Quick, Para,' they said, 'you take his head.'

'I instantly went and held the man's head; he was dressed in army camouflage gear, and covered in mud and blood. The students were cutting up the leg of one of his trousers, and pulled back the cloth to reveal not his shin, but a total mash of blood and bone. I nearly fainted, but didn't dare.

'It was too dark to see much, but even I knew that we couldn't light a lantern, in case it attracted the government soldiers to the house. One of the students stoked up the cooking fire, so anyone outside would have thought we were just boiling some water for tea. The water was boiled, but no tea was made—instead it was used for cleaning the wound. The poor man—I had worked out he was a soldier from the Tamil Tigers—must have been in excruciating pain as they cleaned and dressed the wound by the flickering firelight. He was groaning quietly, his hands clenched and his head far back in my lap with his mouth open so wide I was scared he would scream and alert the government soldiers who were on patrol and passing the houses all the time. My new housemates gave him a rolled-up piece of cloth to bite on.

'They got to work, cleaning out the wound and putting the leg back together. They were so deft I thought, these can't be ordinary students, and later discovered they were all medical students, some of them in their final year. Later, once they had finished attending to the Tiger, they put him in my room to sleep. Then we boiled more water, and I helped them to quietly scrub the blood off the wooden floor and clean away all the evidence. Then, finally, I lay alongside the wounded soldier and tried to sleep, listening to his ragged breathing. What an introduction to university life!'

The next morning the students asked Para to dispose of the bloodied sheets and bandages.

'I nearly died of fright, then realised they were all teasing me,' he says. 'Instead, one of them pushed the material deep down in his backpack and told me he would "lose" it in the hospital incinerators. Then off they went—looking like the carefree final-year medical students they should have been. I felt dizzy with lack of sleep, fear and exhilaration at having helped someone, pride at my fellow students and uncertainty, bordering on terror about the future.

'University was turning out to be different from what I had expected. But that was the first day over with, and surely now things could not be as challenging. Or so I thought.'

Milling nervously through the hall with the other first-year students—his 'batch mates'—to the Arts Faculty for lectures, Para was trying to blend in and not be noticed when he heard: 'Paheertharan Pararasasingam. You are wanted at the front entrance.'

Para was surprised to be called by a senior student and thought there must have been a mistake. 'But he stood waiting for me, so I followed him. There, waiting just outside the entrance and being watched carefully by the security guards, was my dad's brother, Uncle Veliah who worked as a bus driver in Jaffna. I was delighted to see him but also worried—what had happened?

'"What do you think you are doing?" he shouted. I replied that I had just arrived in Jaffna after a long trip from the Vanni and was about to start my first lecture. "No, I mean what are you doing at demonstrations? Don't you know how dangerous this is?" And he pulled a newspaper from under his arm and opened it to show a big picture of me underneath a banner proclaiming "Jaffna University condemns the killing of Mylvaganam Nimalrajan".

'I told him I had just gone along with my new housemates and wasn't really involved. But I could see he was really scared for me, and with good reason.'

Para remembered that Veliah had narrowly escaped when his own brother, also a bus driver, was shot dead at the bus station by the army a few years ago. Para knew Veliah was brave because he still drove a bus each day.

'Stop this behaviour at once!' Veliah shouted. 'Leave the hostel and come and live with me in Jaffna.'

Para told him that he had to organise his ID papers before he could do anything, so Veliah left him with his address and some money.

'I did not want to live outside the campus, so I stayed in my house with the medical students,' Para says, 'but a month later I visited Uncle Veliah and his family and met my young cousins. For the next four years, I saw them frequently and we became very close. Uncle Veliah was very generous—he bought me a motorbike, and at the end of my studies he paid for the graduation ceremony. He was always kind, and very good to me, but he never liked my involvement in student politics because he thought it would bring trouble and danger.

How right he was.'

9

STUDY, ACTIVISM AND LOVE

Para quickly adapted to university life—he loved the lectures and thoroughly enjoyed learning.

Back when he was six or seven years old, his father had insisted that Para and his brother read the news to him by the light of the kerosene lamp.

'Panneer did not enjoy the political reports—he found them very boring—so he would read aloud the other news then slide the paper across to me to read all the news about the government,' Para says. 'At first, I read without understanding a word, but after a while I began to recognise the names, and then the various parties, and slowly I started to appreciate how government worked. Before long I had a good knowledge of the political systems.

'This all really helped at school because in the LTTE-controlled areas the LTTE education wing organised free extra tuition and practice tests in all subjects for Tamil students before they sat the national examinations. They also implemented a compulsory general knowledge test, with 30 percent of the questions requiring knowledge of the

LTTE, its history and achievements. Because I was always reading the papers to Dad, and had become interested in current affairs, when I was about nine years old I easily came top and was awarded a certificate signed by Mathaya, then vice president of the LTTE. The prize for the top scoring students was a trip to Batticaloa, which was amazing for me as until then I had hardly been outside our village.'

The legacy of all this was that Para remained interested in politics and read every newspaper he could find.

Another legacy was that when he reached university and the students were called to action, he found himself unable to refuse.

'At the time, many students were upset by the government. For years and years Tamils had been displaced from their homes and villages by the army, and were living in refugee camps because their homes had been taken from them and occupied by Sinhalese people. Tamils were murdered, raped and tortured. Tamils were disappearing. There was never any justice—if bad things happened to Tamils, that was that.

'Something had to be done about this.'

It was not surprising that Para and his friends would soon become involved. Educated, intelligent and resourceful, students often find it impossible to ignore injustices. United they have the courage—and often the recklessness—to try to make a difference.

'One person could not fight a whole government,' Para says. 'A single person would have been targeted and killed. We saw that happening all the time when journalists tried to stand up to the government.

'But if a big body of people would stand up for justice together, that was a different matter. Like the birds that fly close together in large flocks as protection against the hawks, and the schools of fish that swim in their thousands to avoid the sharks, there was safety and force in numbers. Who better to stand together for justice than university students? Many of us felt it was our responsibility to take steps to stop the army from bullying the minority.

'It was not so much a matter of who was a Tamil and who was not. We believed it was more relevant to see who was oppressed, and who was not. Tamil, Sinhalese, LTTE member, man, woman, child, rich person, poor person—at the end of the day we are all people. It just happened that at the time many men, women and children were persecuted only because they were Tamils. Jaffna University was the main student body that could represent all Tamils, and speak for them, so I felt compelled to do my part.'

During his second year at university, studying hard and working as secretary of the Arts Faculty, Para met Jayantha. A large group of students had travelled to the outlying areas to work with poor communities of Tamils. Squashed in on the bus, Para found himself next to a girl who, like him, was studying economics.

'It was not appropriate for the male students to speak with females, but we were all on the bus, there was nowhere else to sit, and … she was very beautiful!' he says. 'I introduced myself and we started talking. I was surprised to learn that Jayantha did not know anything about politics, or why the LTTE were fighting, or how the Sri Lankan government was treating the Tamils. I told her she should make it her mission to know about these things.

'Then I asked her what she intended to do after university. She told me that her parents had arranged for her to marry her cousin who was living in Canada, but that she did not like him, and neither did she want to go overseas. I was shocked that her fate had been decided so early in her life, and I wondered if there was anything she could do to change things. She replied that unless she married someone in Sri Lanka, then she would have to leave.'

At that moment, looking at Jayantha with her deep-brown eyes, her lustrous black hair and her perfect smile, Para's world fell silent. The noise of the creaking old bus engine and the excited chatter of a hundred students faded as Para fell totally in love.

Then he heard a soft voice, which he recognised as his own.

'Well, would you like to marry me then?'

No more words were spoken. For two months, they saw each other only across the lecture halls or in crowded corridors. Para told a few close friends that he had fallen in love with Jayantha and asked her to marry him, and they mostly laughed at him. He was so busy studying and working in his role of Arts Faculty Secretary that he didn't have the time to think about what had happened.

Then one day, while he was working in the union office, Jayantha came to visit him.

'Are you here on student union business, or a personal matter?' he asked, then wanted to kick himself for sounding so formal.

Jayantha told him she would like to speak with him privately. This was difficult because culturally it was not acceptable for men and women to stand or walk together unless in a group, but they managed to find a secluded place in the hall.

'I have come to tell you that I have spent the last few months thinking about your proposal,' Jayantha began. 'I have asked many people about you—I even spoke with people from your community in Thenmaradchchy, where you grew up. Everyone tells me you are hard-working, honest and a good person. I would like to marry you, but there will be many problems.'

Overwhelmed and delighted, Para could not imagine what the problems could be, until Jayantha told him that she came from a high-caste family, and her parents would definitely oppose the marriage.

'We will be shunned by both our communities,' she said. 'We cannot marry until after we have finished our studies; I must not be seen speaking with you while we are here studying, so we will have to communicate by letters. I expect my parents will disown me for a while because I have chosen someone below my caste. Knowing these problems, do you still want to marry me?'

Para could barely speak for happiness, but he managed to say, 'My first priority has to be to my mum. If you will give her respect, then I am very happy to marry you.'

For the next three years, the couple kept their promises and their secret. Para was only able to communicate with Jayantha through notes and letters. They could talk when they finally procured mobile phones, but they had to exercise great caution to avoid discovery.

'I used to go to the gate at the back of Jayantha's hall of residence,' Para recalled. 'Men were not allowed inside, of course, and we should not have even been speaking, but we still met and talked. We always carried notebooks, so if anyone came along we were able to exchange these and make it look as though we were simply sharing notes from the lectures.'

* * *

By the end of his second year, Para was well known among the students. While he had developed a good reputation from his work that year as secretary of the Arts Faculty, and demonstrated his skills in leadership and public speaking, it never occurred to him that he might become the president of the student union.

Few students were brave enough to undertake the heavy workload of president. In addition to being responsible for student welfare across the university and representing the students' needs to the lecturers, the president's duties included organising social and community projects such as blood donations and community health projects, and working with representatives from the Sri Lankan Monitoring Mission, the multinational body engaged to monitor the ceasefire between the Government and the LTTE. The president needed good communication skills, a strong following from the students and a determination to work for the Tamil community, helping people who were badly affected by the security forces. And, more scarily, the president was expected to work alongside members of the Sri Lankan government and army. And the LTTE.

'In my role as secretary of the Arts Faculty, I had been working in the student union office, helping to prepare for the election of the next president,' Para says. 'Kajendran was the outgoing president; he came from Vanni, had been a strong student leader and was sympathetic to the LTTE.'

To his great surprise, and with little notice, Para was suddenly asked by the LTTE to nominate for the president's position.

'I was completely shocked,' he says, 'but I knew I had done a good job as Arts Secretary the previous year, I was supported by the past presidents, and they believed I could gather support from across the university and unite the students. For the next two weeks I worked hard, campaigning for votes and explaining why I was a good choice. When the votes were counted, we learned that I had gained enough to become the president.'

Para led the six thousand students of the University of Jaffna through one of its more turbulent periods after becoming president in June, 2002.

He had helped to arrange an event in support of the Tamils' right to self-determination in January, 2001. Pongu Tamil (Tamil Uprising) started as a peaceful protest against the disappearances, mass murders and abuses under the Sri Lankan government's military rule. Around five thousand people attended, even though the event was banned, the area was controlled by the army and the police threatened protesters with intimidation and death.

'In 2003, we held the event again,' Para says, 'and this time over one hundred and fifty thousand people came. Many were people who had been made refugees after being uprooted by the Sri Lanka Army, who had taken over their homes to create high-security zones. I read out the Pongu Tamil Declaration to the assembled crowds. Here it is translated:

The Power of Good People

It's more than sixteen months since the signing of the memorandum of understanding. But normalcy has not been restored yet. The negotiations have been suspended. The clouds of war have once again appeared on the horizon, through no fault of ours. We wish to change this situation. With this objective in view, Tamils have gathered here from all parts of the Peninsula, from all its nooks and corners, to freely participate in this Pongu Tamil celebration. We wish to proclaim to the world:

- That we are no longer going to tolerate being pulled about hither and thither or any further dilly-dallying. We wish to get back to our own homes; therefore, the occupying forces must get back to their own homes to enable us to live in ours.
- We wish to build up our normal lives again. To enable us to do that, an interim state structure possessing full powers must be entrusted to the Tamils' sole representatives, the Liberation Tigers of Tamil Eelam. The international community must recognise this interim state structure. The North and East are the traditional homelands of the Tamils. The Sri Lankan Armed Forces must move out of the Tamils' homeland and get back to their own homes.
- The Tamil people are not in a frame of mind to think about peace while being subjected to military oppression and living in an atmosphere of fear. A situation must be created whereby the Tamil people can, in an atmosphere free of fear and insecurity, participate freely and fully to bring about peace.

In such a conducive atmosphere, the ethnic conflict can be resolved in the basis of the following fundamental aspirations of the Tamils:

- recognition of the Tamils as a distinct nation

- recognition of the traditional homeland of the Tamils
- recognition of the Tamils' right to self-determination

It's only on the basis of the acceptance of the fundamental aspirations of the Tamils that a just, honourable and final solution can be arrived at through negotiations and permanent peace prevails.

Noble are we all. All of us are children of the mother earth
No longer prepared to be humiliated, we shall hold our heads erect.

'It was a massive day,' Para recalls. 'I was delighted that we had so many people attending, and it all passed off peacefully because I had negotiated with the army, the police and the LTTE to make sure that nothing could go wrong and there would be no fighting or trouble. The students and the people all worked tirelessly for peace and freedom.'

* * *

On 25 March, 2004, prior to the parliamentary election, the students from the University of Jaffna gathered in readiness to canvass in support of the Tamil National Alliance (TNA). In his role as student president, Para organised buses to transport the campaigning students all around the district.

The students of Jaffna University had decided to support the TNA, which was formed in October 2001 to bring together all the Tamil political parties to contest the parliamentary election on a common platform. In the 2001 elections the TNA had won fifteen of the eighteen parliamentary seats that went to Tamil parties. Soon after its formation the TNA recognised the LTTE as the sole representative of the Sri Lankan Tamils, and supported its struggles for freedom.

That day, Para accompanied a group of around sixty students to a place called Kokuvil, a suburb of Jaffna, about five kilometres from the university.

'In hindsight, this was quite reckless because we were not really safe when we were far from the university,' he says. 'But we felt it was our responsibility to campaign in support of the Tamil party.'

In Kokuvil they knocked at people's houses and asked them to support the TNA in the upcoming election. 'We were handing out leaflets and talking with the local people when I heard army trucks approaching and saw they were escorting the paramilitary group, the EPDP—Tamils who supported the government. We students thought the EPDP were traitors to the Tamil cause and there was often fighting between us. They felt that, as student leader, I was a particular problem.

'As soon as they arrived they snatched our TNA leaflets away from the students and threw them on the ground. The students, mainly girls, argued with all the soldiers, who started to beat them, so I intervened angrily, telling the men they were supporting a government that killed its own people. Suddenly one of the EPDP men recognised me and shouted, "Here is Para, let's kill him!"

'The students realised something was going to happen so they stood in front of me to protect me, but then the EPDP members started beating everyone and the army fired shots into the air so everyone started running. Two soldiers grabbed me and threw me into their vehicle, but the students came back and fought with the army and threw sand at them, which gave me a chance to run.'

But in the melee, another EDPD member managed to hit Para hard on the side of his head with his gun, at which point Para fell to the ground, unconscious.

The news spread quickly and students from all over the district raced to the scene. Many people were injured in ensuing fighting before the army and EDPD left. When it quietened, everyone discovered that Para was missing, and they thought he had been killed or taken. The tension rose as the news broadcasts reported that he had been killed.

'Luckily, however, after I had been knocked out, a lady had come from a nearby house and dragged me inside, locking the door after her,' Para says. 'It wasn't until the fighting stopped that she went outside and told the students she had someone in her house. Then I was picked up and rushed to the general hospital for treatment.

'When they heard what had happened, the students were angry and blocked the main road in protest.'

Fortunately, Para was not badly injured, and was able to leave hospital a few days later.

* * *

In addition to organising rallies and protests, Para was committed to helping individual students with their problems. Gowri came from a particularly poor family. Her father could not find a job because he had lost a leg in a landmine accident, and Gowri had three more sisters who would need to pay for their education.

'Her clothes were threadbare and she could not afford stationery, but she was a very bright and good student,' Para says, 'so I asked the LTTE if they could help her to find a job while she was studying. They were sympathetic and offered for her to receive monthly payments, but by then she had returned home because she had no money to stay in Jaffna.'

So Para was determined to visit Gowri to tell her the good news.

'She lived in an extremely remote area—there was not even a road to her village—so I left my bicycle and walked for the last few kilometres. Her house was very poor; there wasn't even any sugar for the tea. I gave her some money from the LTTE—two thousand rupees—so she could buy some food for her family, and I told her she could start a job with the political wing of the LTTE. This saved her, and her family. Much later I heard she had gone overseas for further studies, and she was married. I was glad to know that she had escaped from such dire poverty.'

At the same time, Para helped students to arrange passes so they could travel through LTTE-controlled areas to visit their families, and he also arranged employment for students living in Jaffna who were far from their homes and families. When the hospital ran out of blood, as it frequently did with all the trauma cases from the war, Para would arrange for the students to attend and donate their blood. He also organised students to visit the war-affected areas to conduct classes for the orphans and children whose families, schools and homes had been destroyed.

But activism, poverty and war were not all they had to contend with. Very early on Boxing Day morning, 2004, a massive earthquake in Indonesia set off a tsunami that tore across the Indian Ocean and slammed into the Sri Lankan coastline, bringing huge waves—as high as 30 metres—and devastating the coastal areas. An estimated quarter of a million people lost their lives in the disaster, with thirty-five thousand Sri Lankans killed and more than half a million displaced. Thousands are still missing.

In an urgent appeal to Tamils around the world, TamilNet reported the Tamil Rehabilitation Organisation's call for help: 'Eight thousand in the northeast of the Island of Sri Lanka ... beaches are strewn with debris and waste. Whole villages have been turned into cemeteries. More than 500,000 have been displaced from their homes and left without shelter.'

Para, as student union president, responded quickly.

'As soon as we heard the news, we students visited Vadamaradchi East area, where thousands of people were affected. The LTTE organised us to bring the dead bodies from the shore to a school so their relatives could try to identify their loved ones. It was a terrible time, seeing people's stricken faces. So many families lost mothers, fathers, children, brothers, sisters ... the LTTE collected the orphans and took them to orphanages. The leaders had a strict rule that the orphans would not be recruited for war purposes.

'After two days helping there, we went to Mullaitivu, where again many people died. We stayed for two weeks, organising temporary shelters and food, water and medical facilities.

'I will never forget that time,' Para says. 'After twenty years of war we had already seen so much death and destruction, but this was on such a massive scale that it was hard to believe

Sri Lanka could ever recover from this natural disaster, on top of the years of fighting. I often think about those poor people who lost everything, including their families.

'Life must go on, but these events left us feeling desolate and empty. We were grateful to survive, but we also felt guilty.'

10

TROUBLE STALKS

In December 2004, Para graduated from the University of Jaffna with a Bachelor of Arts (Honours) degree in Economics. Given the amount of time he spent on all the extracurricular activities, this was a great accomplishment and, as he freely acknowledges, achieved with significant help from Jayantha.

'Jayantha would always take extra notes for me if I could not get to class, and she let me know when we had tests coming up so I could revise when necessary,' he says. 'She was a great teacher even then, and always willing to share her work with me.'

It was difficult to share course notes because, according to the strict customs the two were not allowed to talk or meet. Jayantha lived in a women's hostel while Para was either living in the share house, or staying in the men's hostel on the other side of the campus.

Ingenuity was required. Using a complicated and trusted network of friends, Para and Jayantha managed to exchange notes and messages to arrange meetings at the women's hostel gate. Jayantha would pass the notes she had taken for Para through the railings, and quickly tell him about extra classes or tests that were coming up.

Para still had to do the work for himself, but Jayantha's concise style and explanations helped enormously. If he found anything too difficult, he would then ask the senior students to explain. Everyone knew that he had enormous commitments as president, so the other students were willing to help him keep on task with his studies.

'It was a hard three years for me, trying to manage the students' commitment to supporting the people in these difficult times, trying to keep communications open between the key players in both the army and the LTTE—all the while making sure I completed all the assignments and studied enough to pass the exams. I feel guilty looking back because I know that I often neglected my mum and grandma. It was almost impossible to travel to see family in those difficult years, and I had so little time to spare.'

The final exams were gruelling, but both sailed through and Para became the first person in his family, and from his village, to graduate from university.

However, the honour of being student union president had brought with it a raft of dangers, including threats to his life. Escalation in hostilities between the army and the LTTE now meant it was not safe for Para to even leave the university grounds, so he remained in the hostel. Round-ups and kidnappings were commonplace, with Tamils constantly targeted, and disappearances were everyday occurrences.

Para and Jayantha attended their graduation ceremony in October 2005.

'Uncle Veliah, the one who had helped me at the beginning of my university life, told me that he now thought of me as his son, and he was happy to pay all the expenses for the graduation ceremony. We were so grateful, and we invited my parents and some relatives from my side. But since Jayantha had told her parents she did not want to marry the man they chose for her, no one came from her side, which hurt her deeply, and made her very sad. We enjoyed the ceremony anyway, and were thrilled to be finally graduating from university.

'That was the end of my association with the LTTE—I told everyone that now I had finished with politics, I was going to get a job and soon I was going to marry. That was it.

'But I should have known that you can't just leave the past behind, and that trouble was going to follow me for the rest of my days.'

* * *

Trouble was also stalking Jayantha. She had returned to her home in Point Pedro, where family life was becoming increasingly tense. Her parents had been outraged when she told them she wanted to marry Para.

'In our tradition, parents arrange the marriages, so Jayantha's parents were angry when she told them she had found someone else. And they were furious when they discovered I came from a much lower caste. They said that if Jayantha chose me, then all her family and her community would disown her, so she would have to live a life without any family support. They were very strict and they were determined that she would marry the boy they had chosen. But they did not know Jayantha.'

Before long, her parents told her she *must* marry the man they had chosen for her. When she refused, her father confiscated her phone and told her she would be forced into the marriage. Fortunately, a friend dropped in to see Jayantha, so she quickly borrowed her phone and called Para, asking him to rescue her.

Meanwhile, after a year as president, working between the LTTE and the Sri Lanka Army, Para had become a person of interest to the government forces, and they made it known that he was on a list for arrest and questioning. As a consequence, Para felt it wise to avoid any sort of interaction with the army, so he remained in the relative safety of the university, completing student union business, waiting for his degree certificate and looking for a job.

When Jayantha called him, he told her this was not a good time for them to get married because they didn't have their certificates yet and he didn't even have a job.

'But she was crying,' Para says, 'and she told me that she wouldn't marry the man her parents had chosen, she only wanted me, and that if I didn't help her, she would go straight away to join the LTTE and no one would find her.

'I told her I would marry her at once, and that when she left her parents' house she was to bring nothing—no jewellery, no clothes … not even one rupee. I said this because I didn't want her parents to think I was interested in their money. It was only Jayantha I loved.'

So, on 24 March, 2005, the day after her twenty-sixth birthday, Jayantha left home and called Para to tell him she was on her way to the university.

'I met her and then we wondered what to do,' Para says. 'I had not told my parents about Jayantha, and they had also arranged a wedding for me with another girl, so I knew they would be angry too. Jayantha went to stay at a friend's house while I visited my parents.

'When I arrived at my parents' home I was so nervous and anxious that my mum started asking if I was in trouble with the army or a paramilitary group! Finally, I had to tell Mum that I had found a girl I wanted to marry, and I asked if she would accept her.

'This is your life, Para,' Mum told me. 'You must do what you think is best, but first you must speak with your father.'

'Of course, this made me very scared, but I went to talk with him and he said it was okay, as long as the girl was from our caste, because he did not want to make any trouble with anyone. I had to tell him that, actually, Jayantha was from a high caste, and her parents were totally opposed to me, but that we loved each other. He sighed, told me that I always seemed to bring him trouble, then he told me to bring Jayantha to our home.'

Jayantha had to leave her friend's house a few days later, so the young couple braved the dangers of a bus journey and travelled to Colombo, where they stayed in a hotel for a week.

'We had hardly any money,' Para says, 'and it was terribly unsafe there—young male Tamils were constantly targeted and arrested. It was too dangerous to stay in Colombo, so we returned to Jaffna where at least I was safe in the university grounds.

'It was wrong to be together and not married, so we decided we should have a wedding as soon as possible.'

At the time, with the massive campaign against Tamils, people were being driven together in round-ups and detained, often disappearing without a trace, or abducted in sinister 'white van' kidnappings, where anonymous men used white vans without numberplates to abduct people with impunity. From January to March 2005, eighty-seven Tamils were kidnapped and two hundred and thirty went missing in Jaffna alone.

Back in Jaffna, Para knew the army had targeted him for 'questioning', because of his time as student union president, when he had organised many rallies in support of the Tamil cause.

'I had to stay off the streets, so it was left to Jayantha to organise everything,' he recalls. 'We had no money then because we did not have jobs, but my very generous Uncle Veliah loaned us what we needed. I don't know what we would have done without his help.'

They couldn't invite many people because they didn't want the army to hear their plans. And many friends and relatives could not come—because they were living in LTTE-controlled areas, they were not allowed to travel.

Jayantha chose the temple—Selva Sannithi Murugan—because the priest there would allow the couple to marry without their parents being present.

Traditionally, the mothers and aunties arrange the wedding ceremonies, so it was difficult for Jayantha to make all the wedding arrangements because she didn't have any experience. Even so, she managed to buy traditional clothes for herself, for Para and for his parents. The bride's wedding sari is especially important.

'Jayantha's was a beautiful red one,' Para recalls. 'Because we had so little money she had to choose carefully, as the brides keep their saris safely forever, and are dressed in them after they die. I think you can get "long-life saris", which are designed to last, but we couldn't afford that, and Jayantha said it didn't matter, since she would look after it carefully for the rest of her life.'

Jayantha says that she has never been parted from her wedding sari and she checks it regularly, removing it gently from its wrappings, opening it to let it air, and then carefully folding and storing it away. Each time they had to flee from danger, her wedding sari was the first thing she packed. Despite the numerous moves they have had to make over the years, Jayantha's sari goes with her wherever she travels, wrapped safely in her bag.

'On the day of our wedding, Jayantha had to arrange for someone to help her with the special make-up, and she looked so beautiful,' Para says. 'We dressed in the traditional clothes, then we had to drive to the temple. This meant passing several army checkpoints, where they would ask for our ID cards. This could have been extremely dangerous for me, but because we were clearly part of a wedding party, for once the army did not stop us, which was lucky—I kept my face turned away at each checkpoint so I would not be recognised. It was such a relief to finally reach the temple safely, and Jayantha was delighted to see that one of her aunties was there. Sadly, no one else from her family came.

'Jayantha was so worried that I would be spotted and arrested even during the ceremony that she signalled everyone to gather round closely, so that I could not be seen. At first, we were sitting on the ground so we were hidden by our friends and could not be seen by other people in the temple, but when it was time for us to stand in the ceremony, she was very worried about my safety.'

When it was time, the priest told Para to place the *thali*—a long gold thread like a necklace, tied with three knots to symbolise mind, spirit and body—on Jayantha. Then they had to walk around a sacred fire three times, and then they were officially married.

'It was a beautiful moment, but hard for us to concentrate on the marriage ceremony and not think about the consequences if the soldiers recognised me,' Para says. 'Jayantha had arranged the meals after the wedding, which everyone enjoyed, but we could not stay long in case the security forces came.'

It is almost impossible to describe the problems Para and Jayantha faced at that time. They had offended Jayantha's family by choosing each other rather than abiding by her parents' decision; they had only just graduated and had no regular income; the country was embroiled in a difficult and dangerous civil war; every day there was danger from the Sri Lanka Army or the LTTE; and Para was targeted by the army because of his work as student president.

Despite all of this, they counted themselves lucky and happy—they loved each other, had chosen each other and were now married. They were about to embark on life together. What more could they want?

11
WORK, MARRIAGE AND STRIFE

The first task for Para and Jayantha, like any new graduates, was to find a regular job. The situation was dire, with around 90 percent of graduates unemployed and only medical students assured of a position.

However, Para was fortunate to find employment as a field officer for Sanasa Development Bank. He was responsible for the farmers living in the Kilinochchi District, which meant regular trips into the region to meet with the village leaders and farmers to assess progress with loan repayments and to see if the farmers needed any help with getting finance for supplies.

The job would have been enjoyable, and even unremarkable, if the country had not been gripped by civil war. Battle lines changed frequently and areas were fiercely guarded by either army or rebel forces. Para's clients all lived in the LTTE-controlled areas, while he was living in a Sri Lanka Army-controlled area—which meant he had to obtain permission before he could pass through any checkpoints. On every occasion, the Sri Lanka Army soldiers would call

Sanasa Bank to check Para's credentials. But after a few months Para came to know the soldiers from both sides.

'They would smile at me and ask me what was happening in the other areas,' he says. 'The Sri Lankan army wanted to know what I saw in LTTE-controlled areas and the LTTE wanted to know about the situation in the army-controlled areas. It was common for both parties to approach travellers for help and information, but the problem was, if anyone helped one party, then the opposite party would kill them as a suspected spy. So the regular travellers faced many difficulties between the checkpoints and I had to be really careful what I said to anyone.'

Once a month the bank would hold a meeting and workshop in Colombo. This involved many hours of risky travelling and negotiating with soldiers at the numerous Sri Lanka Army and LTTE checkpoints, but Para always attended because bank officials weren't able to access the LTTE-controlled areas themselves, and they looked forward to hearing news from the rural areas.

Journeys that should have taken a few hours often seemed to take forever, as there were so many checkpoints, each involving long queues, suspicious and officious soldiers, and danger at every stage and from every corner. People were often taken away 'for questioning' and never seen again, random shootings were common, and bombs were an everyday hazard, with checkpoints making relatively soft targets. Hundreds of kilometres of railway track disappeared as the sleepers were taken by both sides and used for building bunkers, so buses were the main form of public transport. When Sri Lankans—Tamils and Sinhalese alike—set off on even short journeys, they always wondered whether they would make it back alive.

Para recalled the journey he regularly undertook to see his clients.

'It was necessary to use five separate buses to travel the one hundred and forty-five kilometres from Jaffna in the north, through the LTTE-controlled areas in the Vanni region before reaching the army-held town of Vavuniya. Returning from Vavuniya, we had to walk from the army checkpoint at Omanthai through "no man's land" to the LTTE checkpoint where our ID cards were carefully examined. Then a bus would transport us another five kilometres to the LTTE guard post at Puliyankulam where we would join the LTTE's Tamil Eelam Transport Service to the army barrier at Muhamalai. Then we would be taken to board a bus to Jaffna.

There was no public bus between Colombo and Jaffna. Instead, passengers had to organise ourselves into groups to hire private buses. The fares (about 1,000 rupees, or $US 10) were equivalent to a week's wage. All along the road, the bus carefully drove around the huge holes left by explosions. And on either side there were wrecked buildings—houses and shops demolished in the war, and notices warning "Beware of landmines".'

Although travelling was difficult and dangerous, Para felt lucky to have a job at all. However, the pay was so low that he was simply not making enough money for them to live.

Ever the entrepreneurs, Para and Jayantha noticed that a nearby chicken farm seemed to be operating successfully, and when they discovered there was no farm in their own area, they researched the idea. Before very long, they had purchased two hundred and fifty young chickens with a loan from one of Para's cousins in Switzerland.

'We had absolutely no idea what we were doing,' Para says. 'We looked at these small fluffy creatures that we had just bought and wondered why we had ever thought it could be a plan!'

Yet within a few months the chicks had grown and started laying, and the couple found themselves delivering hundreds of eggs to local restaurants and bakeries. Sitting side-saddle on the motorbike behind Para, the eggs resting in a bucket balanced precariously on her knees, Jayantha would hold on tightly, and urge him to go carefully. By starting very early each day Para was able to manage the chicken farm and the egg deliveries with Jayantha before starting his work for the bank; so life was, for a while, busy yet relatively uneventful.

Then later in 2005 the government fulfilled an election promise and suddenly announced it would offer jobs to thirty thousand graduates.

'We were so pleased that finally we could work in jobs that we had studied for and wanted to do,' Para says. 'Also, we would have the security of a government job, with government ID. But more than that, now we could live quietly and work normally ... or so we thought.

'I had learned a lot at the bank, and we had enjoyed building the egg farm, but we really wanted to teach, so I was happy to hand back my field officer job to Sanasa Bank, and we sold the farm and repaid our loan. Jayantha was appointed to teach at St Fatima's Boys' School, and I was asked to go to

St Mary's Girls' School. They were two Catholic schools in Pesalai, a small fishing town on Mannar Island, in the northwest of Sri Lanka.'

The District of Mannar was controlled partly by the army and partly by the LTTE. 'We had heard there had been many clashes there between the two forces,' Para says. 'The Sri Lankan navy and army attacked the local fishing vessels, because they suspected the fishermen sympathised with and helped the LTTE; and in turn, the LTTE attacked the navy ships, often with suicide bombers, and targeted army convoys bringing supplies from the south.'

In an attempt to keep control, the army operated curfew systems in all Tamil areas, forcing people to stay inside from 9 p.m. until 6 a.m. In an emergency, such as a need to go to the hospital or fetch a doctor, people who ventured outside had to carry a kerosene lamp, held high to show their faces, and go straight to the nearest army checkpoint to explain their reason for being outside.

In Jaffna, packing their few possessions—which of course included the precious wedding sari—Para and Jayantha wondered how this next stage of their lives would unfold.

The country was still at war with itself and every day they heard of new atrocities from both sides. People died in LTTE-orchestrated suicide bombings on crowded buses or in train stations; people were taken aside by the Sri Lanka Army for questioning at checkpoints, then never seen again; people were shot by both sides as they went about their daily business; and government and LTTE soldiers alike held people in secret bunkers, where they were beaten and tortured, often on the slimmest of suspicions.

It seemed as if this long, dark war would never end. But people had learned to be resilient, and mostly they continued their lives, often fearing the worst, but always hoping for the best. They had no choice.

Frequently, the news was terrible and Para would hear of close friends or family members killed or badly injured in an attack from one side or the other. Suddenly the blur that was 'people' would crystallise into a single person who was known, cherished and loved. Then it was especially difficult. But still, everyone kept going.

With this spirit of stoicism, Para and Jayantha prepared for their first teaching job.

'On the first day, we awoke very early in the morning, packed our few possessions on the motorbike and started our journey to Mannar District,' Para says. 'Firstly, we had to stop at the army checkpoint in Mukamalai. The soldiers were full of questions—why were we travelling, where were we going, why were we going there, did we have authorisation? We explained everything and showed our letters of appointment.

'It took ages, and this was just the start—we discovered there were ten checkpoints to get through, with each one as thorough as the first. Every army checkpoint was an easy target for the LTTE, and attacks were frequent, so stopping and waiting in line was always stressful. As well, people were commonly taken aside by the soldiers for "further questioning" and never seen again. We felt very vulnerable on our motorbike and Jayantha said we should travel by bus in future.'

Finally, they arrived at the Zonal (District) Office in the town of Mannar and received their official papers. Then they had to find somewhere to live. It was hard to find a house to rent because they were from outside the area, and people were suspicious.

'That is another sad thing about civil war,' Para says. 'We weren't fighting a common enemy from outside; people had become scared and suspicious of each other. The Sri Lanka navy controlled the area, and the local people were very frightened of them so did not want to do anything that might attract their attention, even rent a room to strangers.

'Finally, a friend helped us to find a nice three-roomed house to share with two other teachers. Then we had to register at the local police station where they asked for our national identity cards, our army identity cards and our job identity cards. These cards were colour-coded to indicate where we came from and highlighted if someone was not local.

'If we did not register immediately, we could have been in great trouble. The details of all the people living in each house were pasted onto the wall outside so the army or navy could call at any time and check that only the registered people were living there. Our details were then routinely shared with the army, the Criminal Investigation Department (CID) and the Terrorist Investigation Department (TID). If there were any concerns, we would then have been summoned to the army camp for further questioning. This would have been terribly dangerous because people who were taken to the camps were frequently "disappeared", never to be seen again.'

Although they were happy living in Mannar, commuting by motorbike each day to Pesalai—where they enjoyed teaching and soon gained the respect of the students and other teachers—Para immediately realised that the peaceful life they so longed for was still going to elude them.

Pesalai was a small fishing village with a large Catholic community, hence the two Catholic schools. At the heart of the town, the Church of Our Lady of Victories had served as a refuge for the community throughout the war. Set right on the water's edge, Pesalai witnessed many on-water confrontations between the LTTE Sea Tigers and the Sri Lanka Navy, and the community had to deal with the violent aftermath each time the government forces arrived, looking for revenge. As a result, local people frequently sought sanctuary in the church.

A few months after they started teaching, on 15 June, 2006, a violent confrontation between the police and the LTTE had resulted in six thousand people seeking sanctuary in the church, and several houses in the town were damaged.

Two days later, early in the morning, a particularly violent clash out at sea involving the Sri Lanka Navy and the LTTE Sea Tigers left more than thirty sailors dead and the navy enraged. The fishermen who witnessed the battle returned with the news. Around two to three thousand frightened villagers—some of whom had lost their homes following earlier incidents—again took shelter in the church.

A group of armed and angry men in navy uniforms arrived and walked down the road, firing indiscriminately into homes. More men on motorbikes arrived at the church, their faces covered to mask their identities. They set a gun on a stand and fired at the church for ten minutes or so, then threw a grenade through a window, killing one elderly woman and injuring many more. The fact-finding mission established after the event reported that:

Eye witnesses spoke of the chaos that prevailed within the church throughout this time; people screaming, crying out, wailing, praying, bullets and shrapnel flying, people being wounded, fainting, crawling to and fro, trying to avoid the bullets and moving towards the altar for greater safety.

... The attackers then moved to the beach ... According to the reports compiled by the Bishop of Mannar based on eyewitness accounts ... four fishermen were lined up and shot through the mouth, as they kneeled on the ground ... the assailants set about burning the fishing boats and the *wadiyas* [the thatched huts in which nets and equipment were stored].

By the end of the day, forty-seven people in the church were injured, with one person killed; five fishermen were killed and one was seriously injured; thirty-nine boats and forty-five *wadiyas* were destroyed. The community and surrounding area depended almost entirely on fishing and associated employment such as rope binding and transport, so with a depleted fishing fleet, the people of Pesalai faced starvation.

The Sri Lankan government forces wanted more, however. They went on the prowl looking for Sea Tigers whom they thought may have been hidden in the villagers' homes, or who had been helped to escape from the area. Suspicious of everyone, they only wanted revenge, and seemed intent on finding culprits, regardless of their guilt or innocence.

'This is the area we were sent to, for our first teaching positions,' Para says. They were twenty-eight and twenty-seven years old.

12

THE MASKED MAN

War surrounded the young couple, with every day bringing new dangers, but like so many others they tried to continue as normal a life as possible. They established a routine: travel to school to teach and tutor their students, shop in the markets for fruit and vegetables, prepare food together and in the evenings mark tests and prepare lessons.

These quiet and happy times were shattered when one morning they were wakened an hour or so before dawn by the frenzied barking of the village dogs.

'Dogs barking meant army walking,' Para says. 'The soldiers would try to creep into the villages before the curfew was lifted at 6 a.m.; that way they could catch people in their homes, because no one was allowed to leave their homes while the curfew was in place. But as soon as they set foot in the village the dogs would start to bark, and that gave everyone a warning—not that we could do much.'

Jayantha was awake at once.

'It sounds as if the army is in the village,' she whispered to Para. 'It's probably just a usual round-up, so let's get up quickly and shower and cook so we can go straight to school when they leave here.'

Round-ups were commonplace. They were always terrifying because anything could happen when angry young soldiers forced their way into a village of defenceless, frightened people, but everyone had become used to them and just hoped for the best.

They hastily jumped up. Para started preparing vegetables and cooking for the day while Jayantha showered. Suddenly there was loud banging on their door.

'Come out, this is a round-up!'

Resignedly, Para turned off the gas while Jayantha grabbed all their ID cards—their army ID, their national ID and their workplace ID. To be found with any card missing would definitely involve a trip to an army camp for 'questioning'. Despite the shouting and barking dogs and general chaos, Para and Jayantha were reasonably calm—they were more bothered by the inconvenience than by a feeling of danger. This changed when they reached the middle of the village and saw how many soldiers were involved, each heavily armed and irate.

'It appeared they were really looking for someone, or for a scapegoat,' Para says. 'It was still dark so we couldn't see much, but they were obviously angry, and there was a lot of shouting and shoving.'

The villagers were told to get into two groups, with men separated from women. Then the women were made to form a line in front of an army truck while the men were told to stand aside, under the trees. By now everyone was tense and scared—the soldiers were notoriously trigger-happy—and everyone knew that anyone could be shot at any moment, with no consequences for the soldiers.

The mothers tried to shush their children; no one wanted to draw any attention to themselves. One by one the women were ordered up to the truck and when they were close enough they saw someone was seated on the passenger side, looking down at them, through the window. The person was dressed in dark clothes, his head swathed in a black scarf so only his eyes could be seen. When Jayantha's turn came, a soldier grabbed her roughly by the arm, half-dragged her to the truck and made her stand in front of the window while the person in the truck stared at her.

'Look at him,' ordered the soldier, and Jayantha raised her head and stared into the dark-brown eyes. After a few seconds, the masked man shook his head and Jayantha, now shaking in fear, was pushed away to join the other women.

This went on for some time until all the women had been cleared. Then it was the men's turn.

Everyone knew that the man in the black mask had been ordered to look at the villagers to see if he recognised anyone or could incriminate anyone—perhaps he was a spy, or an army supporter, or maybe he was himself a captured LTTE soldier, ordered to point out any LTTE members or sympathisers. Whatever and whoever he was, he held the fate of each villager in his gaze. One nod of his head and they would be dragged behind the truck and shot.

By now everyone was terrified—who was this man? In the shadows, and masked so only his eyes showed, he represented a stark reminder of exactly what is meant by 'civil war'. Here was the enemy in their midst—but who was he? He was not an easily identifiable foe; he could have even been from this or the neighbouring village, forced to sit in judgement on his fellow men and women. As each villager was ordered to stand before him, they knew that just one nod could signal their death, regardless of whether they were guilty or innocent—of what? There would be no chance to defend oneself.

By the time Para was ordered forward, his heart was thumping. He knew that there was no reason to single out and shoot him, but in this environment, anything could happen. His work as university student union president had brought some notoriety, his photographs had often appeared in the newspapers, and many people associated him, through his work as a student leader, with being sympathetic to the Tigers' cause.

This man who was now staring at Para had the power to end his life with just a nod of his head.

Their eyes met. The men stared at each other. And stared. And stared. The villagers fell silent; the soldiers, sensing a change in the atmosphere, turned their attention to Para.

'I could only see his eyes; around his head there was a black scarf, like a mask,' Para says. 'His eyes were brown, like everyone's, and I could not see any other part of him, but somehow, I felt I knew him. Everything seemed to stop—the dogs stopped barking, the children stopped crying—at least that's what I remember. Maybe I was concentrating so much, or I was so scared, that I just didn't hear anything.'

Then Para heard the early-morning crowing of the village's cockerels, and felt a trickle of perspiration down his back; although a Hindu, he was working in a Catholic school and knew the Christian Bible.

'I heard the roosters start to crow, and I thought of the Bible story where Jesus says, "Truly I tell you, before this very night, before the rooster crows you will disown me three times" and I wondered if this man was going to nod his head and sentence me to death. I stared into his eyes, and we both knew he had the power to do either. I could not stop feeling that I knew him somehow, and I wondered if in some way I had helped him once, or if I had offended him. He just stared at me without blinking, and we all—me, the soldiers, Jayantha and the villagers—knew that he was struggling to decide what to do.

'It is very hard to stare directly at someone, and I found my eyes flickering from left to right, looking directly into just one of his eyes at a time. I was trying to communicate with him, or maybe even plead, using only my eyes, and he was trying to work out what to do with me.

'In the end, I didn't blink exactly, I just lowered my eyes and closed them for a fraction of a second, so I didn't see him shake his head, but I felt myself being dragged roughly aside by a soldier and told to move away. I thought the soldiers were angry that he had not nodded his head—they really were looking for someone to blame that morning.'

Weak with relief, Para had to retain his composure while the soldiers were looking at each other, trying to decide what to do.

Finally, they took Para to another truck and asked for his ID cards. His heart was still thumping as he handed over everything, aware that his personal ID card was white, which marked him out as a stranger to the district—the colour code for this area was blue. The cards were taken away and Para stood there, trying to appear calm and breathe normally, even though his heart was racing.

A few minutes later, a soldier roughly thrust Para's cards back at him and told him he could go. He noticed the cards were warm and guessed they had been photocopied, but otherwise everything was in order.

Para signalled to Jayantha and the two young teachers left the area and set off for school. He longed to somehow communicate with the masked man, but he knew that would result in instant death for them both—and perhaps also for Jayantha—so he just walked away, sending a silent, heartfelt thank you.

On that terrifying morning, all the villagers passed the 'test'; no one was singled out and killed.

A few days later a man was found dead in a ditch behind a nearby bus station, shot through the mouth. Everyone presumed it was the masked man, murdered for not providing a convenient scapegoat.

'I think he did know me from somewhere,' Para says, 'and I think the soldiers knew that he did, but they had no proof at the time. Because he did not send me to be shot, he ended up shot himself. I will never be able to thank him personally, but he is frequently in my prayers.

'I know that on that day, for a reason I will never discover, the man in the black mask decided to save my life.'

13

THE WHITE VAN

Tensions were mounting in the days following the round-up and the encounter with the masked man, but life had to go on.

Para and Jayantha still had to travel to work each day along the hazardous Mannar-Pesalai road. The most dangerous part of the journey was at the checkpoints where everyone had to stop and wait while the Sri Lanka Army soldiers checked their ID cards. It was common for people to be pulled aside 'for questioning', and the uncertainty of the outcomes made every interaction with the army traumatic.

After every checkpoint followed long stretches of the bumpy, potholed road, which left the slow-moving travellers vulnerable to being shot or kidnapped by soldiers from either the army or the LTTE.

'Every day something terrible happened,' Para says. 'Usually there was no reason, no warning. We did not know how to relax; we had to think and stay alert all the time. This was the reality of the civil war—we weren't part of it, but we couldn't escape it. We didn't like it, but we couldn't change it. We just had to accept it. We all tried everything we could to keep safe, out of harm's way and to not attract attention. The daily news reports at the time were awful—dead bodies were found in ditches with marks of torture, women were raped, children were harmed. But we had to carry on, because that was "normal for Sri Lanka" at that time.'

Para and Jayantha discussed the alternatives. They wanted to continue teaching because that was their vocation and their employment. They knew their pupils were working hard to achieve high scores and proceed to university. But the daily commute to their schools was taking its toll, particularly since the round-up earlier in the week, which had left them both feeling apprehensive and anxious.

Jayantha suggested that they leave the motorbike at home and travel by bus because they knew the LTTE would not deliberately attack a bus, and if the army intercepted it there would be many witnesses if anyone was arrested. But Para preferred to use the motorbike because he thought it was more manoeuvrable and it would be easier to avoid any incidents. Danger could come from either side.

The third day after the round-up, Para and Jayantha had compromised and were queuing at the army checkpoint on their motorbike, close behind the bus, when a massive blast from the trees lining the road ahead threw everyone to the ground.

'A Claymore bomb had been detonated,' Para says. 'Some soldiers died at once, others opened fire in the direction of the attack, although I didn't see anyone in the forest. We all stayed down until it was over, then everyone was told to line up and show their ID. Our ID showed that we came from

Jaffna, so we were told to wait, along with everyone else who came from outside the district. We should not have worried, because we knew we had done nothing wrong and we had government ID because we were teachers. But we were anxious because no one could ever predict what the army would do next.'

At last their turn came. Jayantha's ID was scrutinised and returned, but Para's was taken away and he was told to give his address and his reasons for travelling. Then the soldiers told him they needed a police report, which they sourced from their head office. Finally, all ID cards were handed back and Para and Jayantha were allowed to continue on their way to school.

'It was hard to concentrate on teaching that day,' Para recalls. 'Jayantha had told me she felt unsafe, but we didn't know what to do. We were just young teachers, and like all our friends we were often scared even though we had done nothing wrong. Anyway, we both taught our classes and at the end of the day I collected Jayantha from her school and we set off home. We had tests to mark, so the evening was normal, but we were both still extremely anxious, especially Jayantha. She said she had a feeling something bad was going to happen, but I told her everything would be fine.'

Jayantha had told the house owner that they were upset by the day's events and she had a premonition something bad was going to happen. Everyone was scared, he told them, and they should call out to him if there were any problems. Curfew fell with the dark, so they finished their school work, extinguished the lamps and went to bed for an uneasy sleep.

The white van

Their house was at a junction near two army checkpoints, so they were able to hear any traffic approaching or stopping. All vehicles had to stop at the checkpoints or the soldiers would open fire, but in the middle of the night Para heard two passing vehicles that did not stop at the checkpoints, and there was no gunfire. Dogs barked.

'Dogs barking meant army coming. I guessed something was going on outside, but I did not dare to even look. My heart started thumping again.'

The doors were closed and locked, along with the big outside gate in the brick wall, so they felt marginally safe, but this ended when Para heard the unmistakable whine of an approaching engine that he recognised as belonging to a dreaded white van.

Before he could even think about what was going on, he heard army boots crash-landing in the garden and then a hammering on the door.

Soldiers had come over the wall.

'We clung to each other and Jayantha screamed. We were petrified. Jayantha asked me if we should light the lamp. They were banging and shouting for us to open the door. We knew that sometimes if people opened the door they were straight away shot in the face, so Jayantha was whispering she would open it because they would hesitate if they saw a woman. I told her not to go near the door. After a few attempts, I managed to strike a match with trembling fingers—it took both of us to light the lamp, we were shaking so much. Then I quickly dragged on my shirt but I couldn't fasten the buttons—my hands were trembling so badly. Jayantha was screaming and screaming for help but none of our neighbours came—they couldn't, because of the curfew.

'Jayantha called out so they would know there was a woman in the house, and she asked them what they wanted. They yelled back that they wanted me. She said, "Who are you, what do you want with my husband? We are teachers, we have government ID, we'll come to see you tomorrow."

'They replied, "We don't have to tell you anything. Now open this door!" When I took the key and unlocked it, they pushed inside and grabbed me, then dragged me outside. There were lots of soldiers, and they moved in from all around. That was why the dogs were barking—soldiers had been quietly surrounding the house in case I ran away.

'Then I saw the white van waiting there and my legs almost buckled. The back door was already open. It had no numberplates. The soldiers pulled my arms behind me and tied them tightly, then they tied my feet together and put a rough blindfold over my head. After that, I was picked up and thrown onto the floor of the van. I thought, This is it. I am going to die.

'Two soldiers climbed in and sat on either side of me. The doors were slammed shut and off we went, driving crazily. I tried to keep calm and figure out where we were going, but it was hard to even breathe—the van stank of blood, vomit and faeces. What had happened in there? Who had been in there before me?

'I could tell we were going along the main road, then from the noise and the bouncing I knew we were going across Mannar Bridge. "Not left, not left," I prayed, because that was the way to the big army camp at Thalladi.

The white van

'We turned left.

'I was lying face down, my hands tied tightly behind my back, my face banging on the metal floor of the van. I couldn't protect my head. As the van drove wildly along the dirt road, I slipped and slid across the floor, and the soldiers pushed me back with their boots. It was dark, and my face was covered with a rough, stinking hood. I was crying by now; the soldiers were talking in Sinhala so I did not understand anything.

'Then, after more crazy driving, we lurched to a stop. There was a sound of a gate opening, then we went through it and on the other side the van's door was yanked open and I was dragged out, my arms and legs were untied, the hood ripped off my head and I was picked up and thrown down through an open door. I couldn't see a thing; it was pitch dark, completely black. I landed on top of someone. I was in a bunker.

'It was so dark in the bunker that I literally couldn't see my hand in front of my face. I felt there were several men in there, maybe six or seven, and someone said, "Who are you? What have you done?" I told him my name and said I was a teacher, and I hadn't done anything.

'"Then why are you here? I heard there was a bomb attack today, were you involved?" Again, I told them I was a teacher; I was at the checkpoint when the bomb exploded, but I was only on my way to school. They kept asking me questions about the bomb, but I had nothing to tell them. I heard later that the army would put spies in prison cells like this one. They would be friendly with the prisoner and pretend to help, but really they were trying to get confessions.

'I was terribly scared, but I was even more afraid for Jayantha—what was happening to my precious wife? She was

Para's family, L-R: Panneer, Pugalini; his mother, Rani; Grandma; his father, Pararasasingam; Para (aged 11). Para always stood as closely as possible to his grandma, 1989.

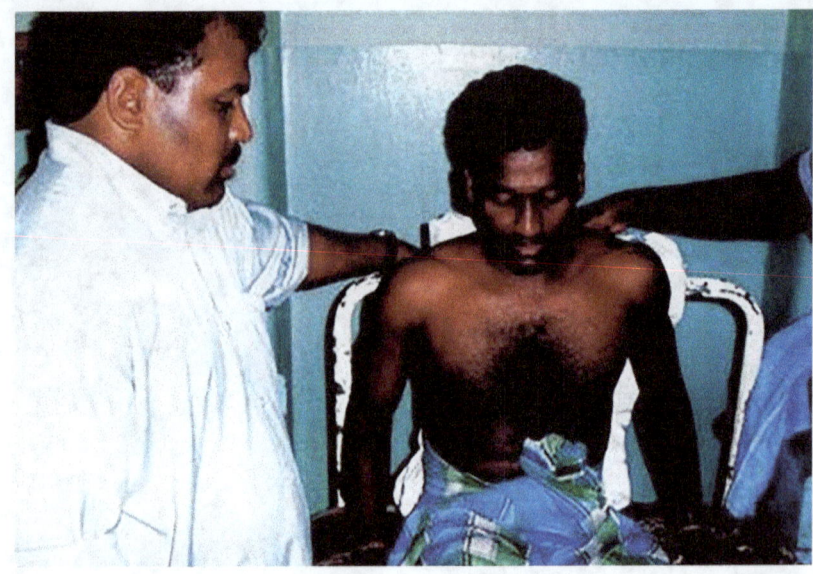

S. Gajendran, former President of Jaffna University Student Union, visits Para in hospital following an attack on Para and other students by members of the Eelam Peoples Democratic Party wielding clubs and poles.
Source: *TamilNet*, 25 March 2004.

Para and Jayantha at their wedding, 28 May 2005.

Para and Jayantha's graduation, Jaffna University, 6 October 2005.

Celebrating *Vidyarambam* with Jayantha and Abi in Chennai just before Para left for the boat that was to take him to Australia, October 2009.

The fishing boat carrying 39 people (incl. 3 crew members) starting to sink in the middle of the Indian Ocean about 30 days after leaving the Indian port of Mangalore. Photo courtesy Steve Hardie, crew member of the *LNG Pioneer* gas tanker that saved survivors, 1 November 2009.

The little boat quickly sinks as the sun sets. Many could not swim and gale force winds blew throughout that night, creating mountainous waves. Photo courtesy Steve Hardie, 1 November 2009.

Members of the *LNG Pioneer* crew helping survivors from the inflatable life raft onto the rope ladder – a dangerous and exhausting operation for everyone, that went on for many hours. Photo courtesy Steve Hardie, 2 November 2009.

Master, officers and crew of *LNG Pioneer* after the rescue, 3 November 2009. Photo courtesy Andy Hill.

Para, a proud Australian citizen with Alison. Photo courtesy Pam Hutchinson Photography, 26 January 2017.

After two years in detention and eventual release into the community Para was still not able to see his wife and son because they were living in Sri Lanka. They managed to reunite briefly in Singapore in 2015, after a separation of six years.

In 2016 Jayantha and Abi moved to India, enabling Para to visit them twice. For the first time, Para was able to take Abi to school. Chennai, March 2017.

left at the house with all those soldiers. What were they doing to her? Beatings? Rape? Torture? Anything was possible. We had recently been delighted to discover she was pregnant, but what was happening to her now? Thinking about this, I didn't really care for myself any more.'

Para should have had more confidence in his brave and intuitive wife. When she was at school that day, Jayantha had confided to the priest that she was very scared—the round-up and then the bomb blast had brought them unwanted attention from the army, and she had a feeling something was going to happen.

The priest listened sympathetically—he had seen this sort of thing many times before. 'You will be safe,' he said, 'I'm sure nothing will happen to Para because if a teacher is attacked and harmed then all the teachers will leave the district and the government doesn't want that.' But he was sufficiently anxious to give his mobile phone number to Jayantha.

So the moment the soldiers left, following the white van, and the military trucks roared away, Jayantha called the priest. It was three o'clock in the morning, but despite the curfew, he came at once. He was in danger of being shot by either army or LTTE soldiers, so he wore his vestments and held his hurricane lamp high. He had to pass through two checkpoints, but he arrived safely and took all the details from Jayantha, then phoned the Bishop of Mannar to ask for help.

Hearing the priest, the neighbours came carefully to the house and apologised for not coming out to help, but Jayantha knew they could not have done anything and would probably have been shot themselves. They stressed that Jayantha must stay inside and lock the doors, and call out if anyone

The white van

returned—they were all worried the soldiers might come back now that they knew Jayantha was on her own.

Back in the bunker, two men continued asking Para questions about the bomb blast, and he continued telling them the truth—that he knew nothing. Then the heavy bunker door was unlocked and yanked open. Several soldiers stood there, shining their torch on every face, letting the beam linger on each one until they came to Para.

'You, come with us,' they ordered.

The men in the bunker said, 'That's it, you're going to be shot. They've shot ten people in three days. Now it's your turn.'

The soldiers dragged Para out and proceeded to beat him.

'I don't know how many people beat me,' he says. 'It didn't stop. Fists and boots. My body, my back, my head, my ears. When I fell down, they just kicked me with their army boots. It seemed to go on forever. They didn't say anything—they were too busy hitting me. Then they just threw me back in the bunker.'

Outside the camp, the priest and bishop were working quickly. The bishop called the commander of the camp.

'Why did you take this man? He is just a teacher; he is not an LTTE soldier or a spy. I can vouch for him. He comes from Jaffna, outside this district, like so many other teachers and government officials. If your men hurt him or kill him, then everyone will leave. You will have no teachers, no planning officers, no top-level staff.'

The commander was left to consider what it would be like the next day without anyone working in any of the government offices. He had to decide whether to allow his soldiers to kill Para. A scapegoat for the explosion needed to be found, but maybe it wasn't too clever to choose this one. He had to weigh up the alternatives.

Lying in the dark, bleeding and semi-conscious, Para was aware of the bunker door opening again, and the same soldiers in heavy boots entering. The same routine with the torch followed, then when they found him on the ground they seized him and dragged him out again.

'I couldn't even stand up straight, let alone walk,' he says, 'so they had to drag me, and one held me up while the other tied my arms and legs and put on the blindfold. There was no need to tie me, I couldn't have run anywhere. Then again, I heard the engine of the white van. I knew now for certain that they were going to shoot me and throw me away. I was too tired to think, let alone feel fear, so I just prayed for Jayantha.

'They threw me in the back of the van again and climbed in beside me. My blood was mixing with the dried blood on the floor of the van. I had no idea where we were going. I knew the high-security prison was away to the left all the way down in Colombo, more than eight hours' drive away. We had all heard terrible stories of torture in that place— I didn't want to be taken there. The bridge home was to the right. I didn't know what they had planned for me, but I started to pray anyway: go right. Go right.'

This time the van did turn right, but Para was now filled with a new terror—were they going back to get Jayantha? Was there someone else to arrest?

Bump, bump, bump over the bridge, and straight past the checkpoint without stopping.

'I thought, my God, we're at the Mannar Bus Station. This is close to where they found the man in the mask three days ago. Are they going to shoot me and put me in the same place as some sort of statement?

'The van stopped, the soldiers leaned over me and untied the knots then pulled off the blindfold. The doors opened and they kicked and pushed me with their boots until I fell onto the road. I thought, Okay, this is really it. I expected a bullet in the back of my head, so I curled up in a small ball and held my hands over my ears.'

Nothing happened. The doors slammed shut and the van roared off, its ugly whine cutting through the early-morning silence.

Para's thoughts were a jumble: They've gone. What shall I do? It's curfew so I shouldn't be out in the streets. I really want to get up and run somewhere, but I can't even stand, and anyway, where could I run to? And if I do move or try to get away, I might be shot by someone else. And this is a high-security zone and anyone moving during curfew has to carry a hurricane lamp. And I don't have a lamp. There are some garbage bins over there, perhaps I can get across to them and climb in. But that would look really suspicious. And anyway, I can hardly crawl. Oh, my God, what shall I do? Maybe I'll just stay here until the curfew ends.

So, for the last hour of darkness, Para lay where he had been thrown, curled up and feigning unconsciousness.

'It wasn't hard for me to lie very still, just then,' he says.

As the dark skies slowly took on a pinkish hue, the first sounds of the pre-dawn whispered from the minaret, echoing down the streets, around the shops and houses, across the bus station and, finally, over the huddled body. Louder and louder, the wailing from the mosque called Muslims to the first prayer of the day. Then the Hindu temples joined, with the ethereal music of devotional songs; and soon the Catholic church bells started ringing. Gradually the skies lightened and, as the sun rose, the curfew ended and it was safe to move.

'I thought, well, I don't know about Allah or Shiva or Jesus, but one of them is looking after me,' Para says. 'And I slowly managed to sit up, and I carefully crawled to the bins so I could pull myself up. I couldn't stand properly, but I needed to walk like a normal person and not draw attention to myself. I could only think of Jayantha. What had happened to her? What would I find at home? So I very, very slowly hobbled away.'

Para knew he had to pass two army checkpoints and he didn't have any ID with him, but as he approached the first one, the soldiers standing there just laughed at him and said, 'Oh, you're back are you?' and waved him through. And at the second checkpoint: 'Oh, you're alive—but it won't be for much longer.'

Para limped down the long and bumpy road. Each step was agony, but he was too preoccupied with worrying about Jayantha's fate to care.

'I was almost sobbing, I was so scared for her; I thought too many things, I imagined so many terrors, my head was reeling.'

Finally, in the distance, he could see his house. And then there was Jayantha, standing in the doorway, anxiously looking out for him.

'Jayantha ran down the road towards me; we were both

crying. We wanted to quickly get inside the house and lock the doors forever, but suddenly people were coming from all directions. Friends from my university came, and teachers from the school. Everyone was so pleased to see me alive. Some came by motorbike; some ran up the road. They were all talking at once and saying that they had never heard of anyone being released after being taken away in a white van; that it was a miracle.'

Jayantha immediately called the priest to thank him for his part in the rescue, and Para spoke to the bishop. Their school principals agreed they should both take a few days off work; and then their lives settled down for a few weeks.

Para knows the enormous debt he owes.

'My life was saved by Jayantha, the priest and the bishop. If Jayantha had not thought to ask the priest for his phone number, if the priest had not been brave enough to come out during the curfew, if the bishop had not spent the night talking to the commander at Thalladi camp, persuading him to release me, then I would definitely have been killed. I really want to thank them. I am Hindu, not Catholic, but the priest and bishop saved me regardless of my religion. I suppose that is what real faith means—to help a fellow being.'

Not surprisingly, Para still suffers from frequent flashbacks and nightmares. Jayantha took him to many temples to pray and offer thanks for his safe return to her. At each temple, they were given thin cotton bands to wear around their wrists.

'I must have had fifty bands, but I still felt anxious. It's not easy to forget and recover but I just went back to work. I smiled, I hoped. That was all.'

14

THE LUCKY ESCAPE

A pattern emerged in the first few months of 2005, when there were well over three hundred incidents involving kidnappings and disappearances.

The army would arrive, usually with a sinister white van, and arrest people—usually young men—and take them in 'for questioning', just as they had taken Para.

Distraught families would go to the army camp to complain and plead for help searching for their loved ones, but the army would invariably deny all knowledge of the case and refer them to the police. Then the police would send the increasingly anxious relatives back to the army. The families were met with a wall of silence.

Meanwhile, in the camps and prisons, in secret bunkers and dark cells, the men—and many women—were beaten, raped, tortured, frequently murdered. Sometimes their broken bodies were dumped back on the streets, kicked out of the back of the white vans; more often, they simply vanished.

Thousands of families still grieve today, not knowing

what happened to their sons and daughters, other missing members of their family, their friends and their neighbours.

At the same time, the LTTE retaliated with fury against anyone thought to be helping the army. The campaign that had started so long ago as a journey to equality and self-determination had become a desperate struggle, killing the very people it once professed to help. Like the army, the LTTE's idea of justice was swift, harsh and unforgiving. Unfortunately, it was frequently misdirected—as in all wars, the innocent suffered the most.

To the couple's delight, Jayantha had recently discovered that she was pregnant. Their feelings were naturally tinged with anxiety. Was it wise to bring a baby into this uncertain world? Where should they be living when the baby was born? Jayantha had to consider her options carefully because her blood group was rhesus negative, meaning that her baby might need an urgent transfusion after birth. In this rural area, with emergency access to city hospitals virtually impossible, this was a significant worry.

However, they decided to continue as normal with their teaching and their lives, and trust that things would work out nearer the delivery date.

Soon after that, though, given Jayantha's condition and after the terror of the round-up and the white van incidents, Para and Jayantha decided they should move away from the north. Para had been so active in student politics at University of Jaffna that he was easily recognised—in a civil war, survival required anonymity, not prominence.

They discussed their situation with the bishop, who readily agreed to help them, although he was disappointed to be losing such good teachers.

But moving away was easier said than done.

'We could not just leave—we were living in an army-controlled, high-security area,' Para says. 'Movement was restricted and checkpoints were everywhere. After my release, I knew the army would be furious that the bishop had intervened and they would be watching me closely, with every checkpoint posing dangers for us. With people being arrested and shot for no reason I knew that if the army saw me trying to leave the area they would be looking for a false charge to put against me.'

Para and Jayantha were trying to work out how they could possibly get away when the bishop offered to help them with a plan—they should leave in his car.

'It was risky for him,' Para says, 'but he knew we only wanted to live peacefully.'

So once more they quickly gathered a few belongings. Jayantha packed her wedding sari, of course, but they had to leave many things behind, including all their kitchen pots and pans, as they did not want to draw the army's attention to the fact they were leaving.

'When the car arrived the next morning, we hid in the back and we were driven to the town of Vavuniya, about three hours away to the south. At every checkpoint, the soldiers saw the bishop's car and just waved us through without even looking at the passengers—but each time our hearts were thumping. I will forever be grateful to the bishop for helping us.'

Once safely in Vavuniya the couple went to the bus station and from there travelled to Colombo—a distance of just under 300 kilometres, which took around eight hours because of the poor condition of the roads.

The lucky escape

On arrival in Colombo they managed to get short-term accommodation in a lodge. They had to immediately register with the local police, who asked them suspiciously why they had come to the city. Fortunately, they were able to explain that Jayantha was pregnant, and because of her blood group, they had been advised to move closer to a big hospital with better facilities.

After a month living in the lodge, and with Jayantha now several months pregnant, they needed to find their own house to rent. Para bought the paper every morning and studied the classified section for a house that would suit them. Since the army continued to target people in the Tamil areas, and round-ups were daily occurrences, they decided it would be safer to live in a Sinhalese area.

Para found a suitable house in the suburb of Dehiwala, not far from the railway station. The owners were initially reluctant to rent their house to 'people from Jaffna', but after Para explained they were teachers from Mannar and were only in Colombo because of health risks to Jayantha, the landlord agreed.

When they arrived to look at the house, the neighbours at first were mistrustful of the young Tamil couple and kept asking what they were doing in their district. Fear and suspicion suffused people's thinking—but with increasing LTTE suicide attacks and almost daily bomb blasts, who could blame them? Para and Jayantha managed to ease people's fears by explaining themselves again.

They needed to buy some pots, kitchen items and cleaning materials as they had not had time to pack their household possessions in their haste to leave Mannar. The local shop was expensive and, because they were Tamils in a Sinhalese area, the prices escalated when they entered. But Para decided to shop there anyway in an attempt to establish a good relationship with the community. It was not easy at first—the shop owner was rude to them and demanded to know why they had come from Jaffna. Para gently persisted, explaining again that they were government employees who had come because of possible problems with Jayantha's pregnancy. In the end, they won over the hostile owner, and later even became friends with him, but the prices didn't drop.

'Jayantha was always extremely frugal—we had to be since we had so little money—and she drove a very hard bargain,' Para says. 'She was prepared to walk away if she didn't think she was getting a good deal. But this time, I begged her before we went into the shop to please, please not bargain too hard, since I didn't want to annoy the owner. Fortunately, she listened to me and we came out of the shop carrying a small stove, two saucepans and some plates.

'Then we needed to collect our bags from the lodge, so we decided to hire a three-wheeler auto, and we met the driver, Kumara, who told us he used to be in the Sri Lanka Army.

'Once we arrived at our new house, Jayantha wanted to immediately observe our special Tamil moving-in custom. This involved heating some milk and sharing it with friends. We didn't have any friends because we didn't know anyone yet, so we asked Kumara to join us, so he went home and collected his wife Nilu and their small son Suji. This was the start of a long and dear friendship. We sat together on the floor, each of us with a small cup of hot milk, heated in a tiny saucepan on the flame of our new stove. Although Kumara was Sinhalese and we were Tamils, we became—and still are—very good friends, and he helped us in many ways.'

Now Para needed to find work again. It was not advisable to talk to the Education Ministry in Colombo, because that would have involved explaining why they had left Mannar and, given the suspicious and uncertain times, they felt it was much better to keep a low profile.

Networking with friends from university days, Para was advised to try looking for work in the eastern province, so he travelled to Trincomalee for the day to register with the provincial head office and to see if he could transfer his position from Mannar. He achieved this after an interview, and began working in the office of the Secretary of Education for the Northern and Eastern Provincial Council as assistant to a man called Kulam.

Trincomalee was too far away from Colombo for Para to commute each day, so he moved into a hostel with a few co-workers in a high-security zone in Trincomalee, travelling there on a Sunday evening ready for work the next day, and back again to see Jayantha each Friday evening, arriving home around midnight.

Jayantha had to remain in Colombo alone, but Kumara and his family once again helped, with Nilu and Suji staying with Jayantha every night that Para was absent. The women soon became close friends, overcoming the language barrier by speaking in halting English as well as demonstrating that once politics is removed, Tamil and Sinhalese people can forge lasting friendships.

By now Jayantha was around six months pregnant, and they thought it was advisable to find a suitable hospital for her antenatal care and the birth. Once again, Kumara helped—he drove them, along with Nilu and Suji, to the local hospital. Closely packed in the auto, Para and Jayantha were excited and anxious to know that soon a scan would show them that the baby was well. After the recent weeks, they felt it was good to be doing something normal.

While waiting for Jayantha, Para started talking to a young doctor who turned out to be a distant relative. He recommended that Jayantha attended the Borrella General Hospital, where she could become his patient. This hospital was a long distance away, on the other side of town, and travelling there would involve passing through many army checkpoints, so at first it seemed impossible. But Kumara reassured them that he knew all the roads so well that he would be able to take them in his auto, avoiding the checkpoints.

Everything seemed to be working out at last. And when the scan revealed that Jayantha would be giving birth to a healthy baby boy, they began to hope that perhaps they might after all share a less eventful life.

On 28 February, 2007, Para started work in Trincomalee.

'It was an interesting job that I enjoyed, working alongside people I liked and respected—I could not believe it!' Para says. 'I knew that Jayantha was safe staying in Colombo and I looked forward to seeing her every Friday night. The baby was well and growing and we looked forward to the birth. This "looking forward to normal events" was so new to us. I felt I was finally healing from the trauma of the round-up, the masked man and the white van incidents. And I felt that for the first time in many months we were safe and our lives were normal—at least, normal for Sri Lanka.'

The lucky escape

Once again, events were about to prove Para wrong.

His daily journey to the office involved walking with his friends from the hostel to the staff bus stop, past some Tamil restaurants where they all bought their breakfast. Across the road were some temples and alongside these was a Karuna army camp, from where soldiers would watch the people moving around the streets. The Karuna group were Tamils but their leader, Karuna, had switched alliance away from the LTTE and to the Sinhalese government. 'They were extremely dangerous,' Para says.

The day after his arrival in Trincomalee, Para was routinely stopped and questioned. Because his ID card had a number that identified he was from the northern district he was an immediate suspect, and his papers were all taken and photocopied. But all was well; after that the soldiers appeared to recognise Para and his co-workers, and left them in peace.

Life proceeded calmly for around three months. Then Para's friend took holiday leave and Para had to walk to the bus stop on his own. A new soldier was leaning against the wall of the camp that day, and when he spotted Para, he beckoned him over.

'He was an Eastern Tamil from the Karuna group,' Para remembers. 'He asked me for my ID; I told him it had already been checked. He was a bullying sort of a person and he seemed to be bored, which is always dangerous.

'He had the power to do anything with me and he had the gun, so I handed over my cards and just kept calm and waited, although my heart started beating faster. I looked across at the restaurant but everyone kept their heads down—everyone was watching, while pretending that they weren't interested. At times like this, no one wanted to draw attention to themselves. I did not blame them. It was very scary.

'Then the soldier looked hard at me. "I've seen your face," he said. Then he looked at my ID: "Pararasasingam—I recognise the name. Now, why would I know you?"

'I just shrugged. By now my heart was thundering, but I think I managed to appear calm. He finally let me go, but I knew then that trouble was brewing, and I needed to do something—but what? If I did not pass that way in the afternoon he would suspect me, and if I did pass by, he might well arrest me. I went on to work, my mind racing.'

Para had become good friends with his boss, Kulam, who was horrified when Para arrived at the office and told him what had happened. He knew soldiers could arbitrarily arrest anyone. And arrests always led to questioning, and generally led to torture, imprisonment and often death.

'Kulam told me that he did not have the power to really help me—we were all at the mercy of these Karuna soldiers. But he had a plan—he suggested that I immediately take a week's leave, and go to Colombo.

'He said, "Leave now, don't wait until the end of the day. Don't use the staff bus to return to the hostel, he might be waiting for you when you get off. In fact, don't go back to the hostel at all; he may be watching it. My driver will take you to the railway station—catch the first train that comes, go to any Sinhalese area and then catch another train or a bus to Colombo. Then text me when you are safely home—no matter what time, send me a text so I know you are safe."'

Para quickly called Jayantha and told her: 'I'm coming home right now. I'll be there tonight.' Jayantha instantly realised there was a problem—like so many others, they lived on a knife's edge, keeping important documents with them, ready to respond to danger at a moment's notice.

Para left the office in the back of Kulam's car, heading for the closest station. It took several hours, taking trains going in the general direction of Colombo, to make his way safely home to Jayantha.

Everyone's fears proved to be well founded. At the end of the day when Para's co-workers were walking past the camp, the same soldier was waiting for them.

'Where is Pararasasingam?' he asked. 'I need to see him.' Para was working late, his friends said, and would be passing much later. The soldier waited.

The friends called Kulam to tell him, so when Para called that night with the news that he had finally reached Colombo, Kulam warned him it was not safe to return.

Over the next few days, people from the office were questioned and threatened by the soldiers. They said they did not know Para, or where he could be: 'He lived on the top floor of the hostel; none of us knew him.'

Sadly, several staff disappeared after this incident—either because the soldiers thought they had been protecting Para, or because the Karuna soldiers were always on the lookout to arrest someone.

'Life was a gamble then, every day,' Para says now. 'I look back on my life and I know that I had many lucky escapes. Sometimes in the middle of the night I waken and I wonder how I am still alive. "Why me?" I ask myself. Then I think of all the people who died during the war—so many good, kind, brave and generous people. I hope that their sacrifices were not in vain and that, some day, justice will prevail. In the meantime, I thank those people who helped me to stay alive.'

15

A BABY AND A BUSINESS

One night about a month before Abi was born, Para was having trouble breathing. As a lifelong asthma sufferer, he was used to frequent attacks, but this one was particularly severe.

He needed to go immediately to hospital for treatment, but knew it was not safe to go alone. Jayantha was heavily pregnant and feeling unwell, so they called Kumara. Their loyal friend decided it would not be safe driving a single Tamil male passenger across the town that night, with the checkpoints manned and the soldiers armed and always on edge, fearing attacks from the LTTE.

Kumara solved the problem by taking Nilu and their small son Suji along with Para, having told the three of them to appear as husband, wife and child—with himself as their driver—to avoid causing suspicion. Para sat on the far side of the auto, away from the checkpoint side, so when the checkpoint soldiers shone their torch, they would first see the Sinhalese driver, then the female Sinhalese passenger, then the child. It was hoped they would assume Para was also Sinhalese.

A baby and a business

At each checkpoint Para sat quietly, struggling to breathe yet not wanting to draw any attention to himself, while the Sinhalese driver and his female 'passenger' complained loudly and assertively to the guards, who waved them through without checking Para's papers. This was important because anyone checking in detail could have found links to the round-up and the white van. Suspicion alone was enough to warrant immediate arrest and all that would follow.

Once again, Para had dodged the system. With help from his Sinhalese friends.

'I would love to be able to return to Colombo to thank them,' he says. 'They would always come out in the middle of the night if I or Jayantha needed help. They were such good people, and also very brave.'

With his asthma under control, and with Jayantha now around eight months pregnant, the most pressing need for Para was, once again, employment. Para checked the papers and noticeboards every day, but the war had made jobs scarce, especially for Tamils.

Fortunately, Para heard of an old school friend, Kiruba, who was looking for an assistant in his seafood transport business. Although a Tamil, Kiruba passed himself off as Sinhalese because he spoke the language fluently and moved in Sinhalese circles. Kiruba was pleased to hear from his old friend, and that evening an ancient van pulled up outside their house.

'It was an old hearse, with two seats in the front and a large space behind,' Para recalls. 'It smelled so strongly of fish! Kiruba told me he was looking for an assistant, so within a few minutes the job was mine.

'But first I had to be registered because we had to travel onto the docks each day to meet the fishing boats, and because of the war the harbour was totally off limits unless people had clearance and all their documents, ID cards and passes. Kiruba somehow managed to get me a six-month pass, so that problem was solved, and it also meant I could stay more safely in Colombo for the next six months.

Now I just needed to start work. And it was hard work. At 3.30 a.m. I would get up and Kumara would drive me to Dehiwala train station because it was too dangerous for me to walk at that time—a single Tamil man walking was a target for the police or army. I would catch the 4.30 a.m. train to Colombo main station, then take the bus down to the harbour, where I would meet Kiruba. The fishing boats were returning with their catch—small boats stacked high with plastic boxes overflowing with shining fish, fresh-caught prawns and live crabs. The boxes were displayed on the quay for inspection and then the auction started.

'We walked down the quay, with Kiruba bidding for the boxes of fish or shellfish that he wanted. Each time Kiruba won a bid, I had to document the transactions and take the box to our car. In my big rubber boots, heavy dark-blue plastic apron and thick rubber gloves I looked just like the other workers. Kiruba told me to just keep my mouth shut, and not speak to anyone because people were worried about having Tamils in the harbour—everyone was so scared that the LTTE might attack. The war made people suspicious of everything and everyone.'

By eight o'clock the auction was over then, laden with their boxes, they drove from the harbour in a convoy with the other dealers to the big fish market in central Colombo. There was no time to spare because the vehicles were smelly and dripping seawater, and they had to be off the road so everywhere could be cleaned before 9 a.m. At the big market, Para again had to remain totally silent because one word could have given him away.

'I had to bring the boxes from the old hearse, open them and stand behind Kiruba while he bargained with the wholesale buyers who were working for the restaurants and hotels,' Para says. 'Once a price was agreed, I had to carry the fish to their cars and then bring back the plastic containers. This was always tricky because the buyers often wanted to talk with me and ask me how much we had actually paid for the seafood, but of course, I could not reply. So I kept silent, and I think they thought I was either truly dumb and unable to speak, or just plain stupid.

'This went on for around thirty-five to forty boxes of seafood each day. If any boxes didn't sell, we took them to the fish processing factory where the price was lower, but at least everything was sold. Then at around midday, we took the empty hearse to the seaside, along with all the other seafood transporters, and we all washed out our vehicles, cleaned everything and hung up the work clothes. Still I had to remain silent.

'Finally, I could go home to Jayantha. It was heavy work, but my new ID showing I was working in the harbour really helped me each time I was stopped by the police or army because a harbour pass was so hard to come by.'

The job with Kiruba was not well paid, so with a new baby imminent, Para was always looking for extra opportunities to make money. Looking through the papers every day—a habit that had endured since childhood—Para noticed that house brokers, who helped families coming into the area find houses to rent, appeared to be making a good living, taking one month's rent in each commission. He invited Kumara to join him in a new business, to be conducted outside the fish market's hours.

'Every afternoon, when I returned from the fish market, I would shower and then Kumara and I would look through all the newspapers, searching for advertisements from house owners wanting to lease their properties, and from people looking for a house to rent. If it was a Tamil family, I would speak with them, and if it was a Sinhalese family, then Kumara would negotiate. We were just matching houses to families.'

Soon, Para and Kumara placed a small advertisement, promoting their business and using Kumara's mobile phone number. But this venture came with associated risks.

'We had to be very careful because, remember, there was still a civil war and sometimes LTTE undercover soldiers would be looking for a safe house to rent, enabling them to live in Colombo and plan attacks on the army checkpoints, or aimed at civilian targets such as bus stations or trains. We did not want anything to do with this, so we only took on families with very young children, never groups of adults.'

In a typical arrangement, Para and Kumara would be approached by a family looking urgently for a house.

'I would tell them I was a broker and I would help them, but that I was busy in the morning, so would see them in the afternoon. Then Kumara and I would look through the newspapers and find a suitable house for rent. Often it was a Tamil family looking and the landlord would be Sinhalese, so Kumara talked to the owner while I spoke with the family. If everything seemed to be working out, we needed everyone to meet at the house.

'It was difficult to travel because the police and army would frequently stop people and ask what they were doing and where they were going. We solved this by always taking Jayantha with us—by now she was almost nine months pregnant, so if we were stopped it was easy to say we were taking her to the hospital. So poor Jayantha was driven around Colombo in the oppressive heat in the back of an auto to help us with our new business.

'Fortunately, the families usually liked the house we had found, the owner generally liked the people, and the agreements were signed. We were so pleased when everyone was happy—especially since Kumara and I made around eleven thousand rupees from each transaction. It came just when we needed the money.'

With a baby due at any moment, Para and Jayantha were living alone in Colombo, with no family support and no idea what to expect, let alone what to buy for the baby. Once again, they were rescued by Kumara and his wife—Nilu went shopping with Jayantha, advising her what she would need.

Since they all lived some distance from the hospital and travelling at night was so restricted and dangerous, Para managed to arrange with his cousin, the doctor, that Jayantha be admitted a few days before the birth, while he returned to their house and kept working. He did not want to risk being held up at a checkpoint with Jayantha in labour.

The Power of Good People

Although the baby was due on 9 June, Jayantha felt the following day was more auspicious. The nurses were sceptical, but with characteristic determination Jayantha managed to wait until just after midnight, and on 10 June 2007, she gave birth to their baby son, Abilash.

As promised, Para immediately shared the good news with Kumara, who roused Nilu and Suji so the four of them could travel more safely to see Jayantha. Arriving so early in the morning, they were initially denied entry. But fortunately Para's cousin was on call, and he allowed them in to see Jayantha and the new baby.

His first sight of Abi was a magical moment for Para, and one he will always treasure.

'Abi was lying quietly in a small basket, quiet but wide-eyed,' he remembers, 'just watching the different colours of the dawn sky and looking at his fingers. Jayantha was resting, it was so good to see them both safe and well.'

Then they had to contend with the issues arising from two different cultures.

'In Sinhalese culture, the women instantly shower after delivering their babies, then they are fed with bananas. But in Tamil customs, the women return home and are given a drink of water from boiled rice, soup made from ground coriander leaves and then a shower using warm water containing eucalyptus leaves. By the time I arrived at the hospital, Jayantha had showered and eaten banana—she was not pleased because it was not her custom, but she had to accept that she was in a different place.

'We wanted to return home, but we felt it was not safe taking such a small baby in an auto, so Kumara arranged for us to travel in a taxi with Nilu and Suji so Nilu could deal with any harassment from the army.

'Finally, we arrived home and I arranged to have a week's holiday from the fish market. Then I called my mum and she told me exactly what food to buy and cook—the special fish that would help Jayantha to make more milk, the particular spices … I went quickly to the market with Kumara and we bought everything, then I cooked it. I was so pleased because Jayantha said that if her own mother had prepared the food it would not have been better than mine.

'Her mother was still not speaking to us—which really saddened us, but we had come to accept she would probably never see us again, even though we now had a beautiful grandson for her to love.'

For the first few days Para looked after his wife and their new son. Abi did not sleep at all. 'He cried whenever we turned off the light—he wanted bright and colourful lights, switched on and blinking all night. I would sit with him and read books and the newspaper to him. Jayantha and I would take turns to sit with Abi. It was exhausting, of course, but that's just the way it is with new babies.'

A short while later, two of Para's young cousins from Jaffna came to stay. In keeping with local laws, they had to register at the local police station, and their names were placed on a poster by the front door. They paid a small contribution to the rent, but the best part of the arrangement was that Para felt able to return to work, because Jayantha now had some female company in the house.

'Our neighbours came with small gifts for Abi, and Kiruba also came with his family and left little presents,' Para says. 'We felt very fortunate and special and loved … the bad things that had happened were firmly in the past; maybe now we had Abi we could enjoy a more normal life.'

But life can never be normal during a war and, in particular, a civil war—often, people don't know the enemy and can't be sure of the friend.

16
NOTHING BUT TROUBLE

In October 2007, Abi was four months old when a major bomb blast rocked a main railway station in Colombo, leaving many people dead and many more critically injured.

Kumara was very worried about Para—a Tamil living in a Sinhalese area risked becoming a scapegoat. Explosions were always followed by round-ups as the army sought to reassure the public by arresting and punishing someone, regardless of whether there was evidence to implicate them in the crime. Stories of white van round-ups were rife again.

Although Para was increasingly anxious that he would be targeted, he had to continue travelling to the harbour to work each day, as there was no other employment for him and they badly needed his wages.

Tensions heightened as LTTE suicide bombers infiltrated the city. Known as Black Tigers, they were trained in handling explosives and ordered to attend areas where there would be a crowd of people, whether because of an event, or simply the rush hour. They would then find the busiest spot and detonate themselves, taking with them as many innocent bystanders as possible—Sinhalese or Tamil, it made no difference. The government was trying to stop the terror, but they had little intelligence to work on, so the army simply rounded up innocent Tamils and took them off in the dreaded white vans, hoping this would deter further attacks.

A few weeks later, a huge blast rocked the local bus station, only around 500 metres from Para's house, killing and maiming many innocent people. This time the bombers struck in the evening, around 7 p.m., when the station was likely to be packed with commuters.

'They chose this bus station because it was in the heart of a Sinhalese area, so it was likely that mostly Sinhalese people would be killed,' Para says. 'It was a terrible thing. I had worked at the harbour in the morning but from early afternoon I was at home, playing with Abi. My cousins were also there, and Jayantha. We heard the blast—it was massive, everything shook, then a lot of smoke filled the air. Straight after the blast I called my uncle in Jaffna to tell him there had been an explosion, but my cousins—his daughters—were both okay—I didn't want him to hear about it on the news, to recognise the area, and to worry they had been caught up in the blast.'

Kumara was some distance away, driving his auto, when he heard about the incident. He immediately called Para, advising him to stay indoors, as he knew the army would be looking for suspects, and would take any Tamil they could find.

It didn't take long for them to find Para. The police had already searched their lists of people registered as living in the area and handed this information to the army. The Tamil name alone was enough to attract attention—the soldiers instantly mobilised, came to the house and surrounded it.

'They came to the door, Jayantha opened it and they barged in, asking me where I had been all day,' Para says. 'I told them I had finished work at twelve o'clock as usual, then had come home, taken a shower and stayed there since.

'Just then our neighbours all came and confirmed that I had been there—they knew because I had been walking in the lane behind the houses with Abi in my arms. Our neighbours strongly protested our innocence, but the soldiers said they still wanted to take Jayantha and myself in for questioning, so they took us in separate vehicles to make sure we could not prepare any "stories". It was awful seeing them taking Jayantha and Abi, but I didn't have time to think because they quickly threw me in the back of a car.

'They decided to leave my young cousins alone in the house—they must have been very frightened, but at least they were not taken for questioning.'

Para guessed that from now on, he might be in extreme danger.

'When we arrived at the police station, they took all my identity cards. In Sri Lanka, these cards are all linked to a central database, and I knew that once they checked the system they would see that I had been the student president and everyone thought that Jaffna University had links to the LTTE. Then there was the trouble following the round-up in Mannar, where Jayantha and I had been teaching, and they probably also had some sort of report from the Karuna soldier in Trincomalee.'

Of course, none of this was evidence, but real evidence was not required at that time. Mere suspicion was sufficient to arrest, incarcerate and question people. Jayantha was taken to the women's part of the police station and kept in a cell for three days. She was not questioned, just detained. Fortunately, she was still breastfeeding Abi, so that was one problem less for her as Tamils in custody were not treated well.

In the first interview, the police tried to unsettle Para by telling him that Jayantha had said he was close to the site of the explosion when it happened. Knowing this was untrue on both counts, Para told them that in fact he was standing just behind his own house, telling the eight-year-old daughter of the neighbour three houses down the street that Abi was too small for her to pick up. Para asked the police to check his story with the neighbours, many of whom had been watching. But the police did not.

Then the investigator asked Para about Kiruba—'Who is the man who has been visiting you?' Para told them that he was a friend from school who had offered him work in the fish markets.

Para was then ordered to remove all his clothes. Once naked, his hands were tied to large metal rings in the wall and three men beat him with sticks and metal wires, then they rubbed burning chillies on his face. When they finished, they pulled him down and pushed him into a cage.

'It was a tiny cage. You could not lie down and sleep in it; you could crouch but you couldn't sit. It was very painful. And they started hitting me through the bars. They would grab my hands and smash the stick on my fingers ... then they brought in the records they had on me, from my time in university …

'"How did you get out from Mannar?" "Who helped you?" "What were you doing in Jaffna?" "Why did you travel so much and pass so many checkpoints when you were at university?" They seemed to have details of all my movements and although I knew I was totally innocent of any crime, they were determined to find me guilty of something.

'For two days, they questioned me, hit me and kicked me with their boots. Always the same questions, and I always gave the same answers, which seemed to infuriate them even more.

'Then on the third day they dragged me to a pitch-dark room and left me there, in silence. The whole room smelled of blood, faeces, vomit, urine … and fear. I was still naked. I was sitting on the floor when I heard footsteps coming. It sounded as if several men were approaching, all wearing heavy army boots. I felt sick—what were they going to do to me now? Then three men came into the room. One of them turned on the light and the first thing I saw was the walls—they were streaked and splattered with dried blood. Then I saw that one of the men had a really, really huge stick. They dragged me up, tied my hands to a chain off the wall, threatened me with the stick and started asking questions again, this time about my work as student president.'

'Why did you travel to the LTTE controlled areas?' WHACK.

'What were you doing?' WHACK.

'Who were you seeing?' WHACK.

'Did you work for the LTTE?' WHACK.

'We have details of all the times you passed the checkpoints—who were you seeing? 'What were you doing?' WHACK ... WHACK ... WHACK.

'I told them again and again that I had to co-operate with the LTTE when I was the president—it was a part of the job and one of my responsibilities. People were not given a choice—if you did not co-operate with them, they would shoot you. At the same time, I had co-operated with the army—that was the role of the president. But once my time as president was over, that was it, I graduated from university and I did not have anything more to do with any of them.

'This did not pacify them. The shouting became louder and louder. They were screaming at me and hitting me with that huge stick. I kept falling to the floor but my hands were tied to the wall so I was just hanging there, and they just kept beating me. They were sweating and cursing me, then one of them yelled, "If you don't confess to working with the LTTE we will kill you tonight!"

'I believed them.

'I was coughing blood, falling in and out of consciousness, hanging there helpless. Then, just as I thought it could not get any worse, and I was sure I was already dying, two of them grabbed me, untied my wrists and turned me upside down. I saw that the third man was now holding a large iron rod. He waved it in front of my face and said, "I am going to put this up your arse until it comes out of your throat."

'Strangely, at this moment, I began to think that, after all, I might survive. I had spoken with several friends who had also been tortured in this way and they told me that this "treatment" with the iron rod was the investigator's last resort. If victims managed to bear this, they may be released, because they had not "confessed", and so had not been proven to be guilty. But if they confessed to anything, just to stop the pain, then that was evidence enough for the soldiers to just shoot them.

'Raising the rod, he came closer …

'The pain was indescribable, there was so much blood. This was torture, this was real. It was terrible.

'I don't want to talk about the next few minutes, or it may have been hours … I really don't want to try to recall it.

'I remember thinking, How can a man do this to another person? Then, mercifully, I became unconscious.

'Much later, or it could have been only minutes—there was no way of telling—I started to come round. Maybe it was the next day, I don't know. Anyway, I slowly woke up and found myself lying on the floor of a cell. My body was covered in bruises and dried blood, I felt deep, heavy pains everywhere and I could barely move my legs. Then I heard someone whispering my name and was surprised and so, so pleased to see my friend Kumara looking anxiously between the bars.

'My God, Para, what have they done to you? No, don't try to get up, stay there. I just want you to know that Jayantha, Abi and your cousins are okay, so don't worry about them. Also, my brother knows the head of CID here, and he may be able to help you. Don't worry, my friend, I know you are completely innocent and I will do everything I can to help you.'

'I could only nod my head. I couldn't even smile. I realised I was alive, and I was thankful, but I wondered what was yet to come.'

The following day Para was taken to the prison hospital and some attempt was made to attend to his injuries. Then a day or so later the guards took him to another part of the prison and placed him in a small cell with six others. They asked him where he was from, and which part of the LTTE he supported. But he had no words. This was partly because he thought at least one of these men may be a spy, so anything he said may inadvertently incriminate himself, partly because he genuinely was not a member of the LTTE and so had no information to share, and largely because he was simply in too much pain to speak.

Para soon came to realise that he was a TID/CID (Terrorism/Criminal Investigation Department) prisoner in this massive prison that housed around four thousand inmates. These prisoners were confined to their cells for all but two hours each day, allowed out only to shower and collect their lunch—a bowl of watery rice served on a soft silicone plate which folded and spilled when food was placed on it.

Para was alarmed to discover that all prisoners in the TID/CID area could expect a minimum of seven years' imprisonment, with a probable life sentence. He began to wonder if he could ever escape this latest predicament.

Prisoners were allowed visitors and Kumara returned regularly, bringing news of Jayantha and Abi, and the plan they were all formulating to secure Para's release. It was hard to exchange information, as anyone could have been a spy, so the men spoke carefully in English. Para knew that the TID/CID had to have prepared a case for the court within twenty-eight days, so they all had to move quickly to arrange his defence, otherwise there was every chance Para would simply 'disappear'.

Fortunately, at this time, Para's cousin arrived from the UK. A businessman with British citizenship, he was initially angry when he heard about Para's predicament: 'I told him not to get involved in student politics. He should have listened to me.' But he immediately started helping his young cousin, reassuring Jayantha that he would try to save Para from the secret prison camps.

'Kumara, his brother and my cousin managed to talk to one of the senior CID officers who agreed the case against me was made up,' Para says. 'He said that he would help to have me released, but that I would have to leave Colombo immediately, because if there was a round-up and I was arrested again and investigated, then he would be in trouble. Since round-ups were occurring constantly, and Tamils were continuously targeted, they all thought I might probably not even get to my house from the prison before being arrested again, so we all agreed that I should leave Colombo as soon as possible.

'When my brother and sister—who were then living in England and Switzerland—heard about the arrest and that I had been tortured, they were frantic. They offered to help in any way and spoke with my cousin who arranged the payments that were required to enable me to receive a fair court hearing.'

Kumara visited almost every day, keeping up Para's spirits and carefully imparting news of their progress, speaking in an impromptu code to ensure no one could understand their conversations.

'Kumara would say cryptic things like "Your brother has come from very, very far away to see your wife, I think you know who I am speaking about. Try not to worry because he is planning to make arrangements for you." And I would attempt to work out exactly what he was trying to tell me, without mentioning any names or exchanging any more information.

'Many of the prisoners had no one to help them, so I had to be careful nobody suspected that I had friends who were trying to get me out in case they became jealous and made up something about me to try to influence the guards. So I only spoke to my inmates about my wife and son. They kept telling me that I would be "disappeared" if I didn't get out in twenty-eight days, but I didn't dare to tell anyone I was hoping to be released, because it was impossible to know who was trustworthy and who was a spy.'

At last, Para was called to the prison office for a final interview with the police. His fellow prisoners assumed he would be moved onto the next prison camp since only five percent of prisoners were freed. The interview went on for several hours with the investigators taking Para back over the last few years of his life, from his student days to events in Mannar, Trincomalee—everywhere he had been. The secretary wrote up the notes and Para was asked to sign, but when he saw it was all written in Sinhala he refused, as he did not understand the language.

'Even though I was a Tamil, like nearly all the people in that prison, they prepared all the documents in Sinhala with no automatic translation. The *Sinhala Only Act* meant Tamils often had no idea what was being decided because we simply did not speak their language and they did not offer translations.'

Eventually it was translated for him and he signed. The following day a thin and dishevelled Para was taken in a closed prison van, handcuffed to the other prisoners, to the court.

'My clothes were filthy, but I did not dare to ask for anything. The van was terrible—it had tiny barred windows, and a police escort. When we stopped at a traffic light you could see the people outside, free, in a bus or walking along the street. We all were filled with despair—we had been in prison for twenty-seven days, where it was always dark and gloomy, and dreadful things were happening around us. The natural light seemed bright and everyone outside seemed so happy, while we were so scared and crushed. Then we arrived at the court where my cousin was waiting, along with Kumara, his brother the army commander, Jayantha and Abi.

'I had to wait with the other prisoners in a separate room, then one by one we were taken in to see the judge. At last, it was my turn.

'The Sinhalese judge asked me if I had been involved in any crime. I replied "No". He asked me about my life and why I had moved from Mannar, so I explained everything— although he already had the report in front of him which declared the TID/CID had not found anything criminal associated with me. I didn't know much about the plans my cousin and Kumara had prepared, so I was extremely anxious. I knew I was innocent, but matters like actual guilt or innocence didn't feature at that time in Sri Lanka. They were speaking in Sinhala, so I still didn't know what was happening. In fact, the CID had withdrawn the case, but I didn't realise that.'

Then Para was taken to the back room again and Kumara's brother came and, speaking English, introduced himself. He told Para not to worry, that he had to return to prison in the van, and that he should sit on the far side of the van and look out.

As the vehicle moved out of the gates Para was able to glimpse his 'team'—Kumara and his wife Nilu, his cousin from England, still with an angry face because he had warned Para to avoid risking this very event—and Jayantha, tears streaming down her face, holding Abi tightly. Although the van was moving quickly, and Para only saw them for a few seconds, he did notice Kumara giving a surreptitious 'thumbs up' and he started to believe this nightmare might soon be over.

'Back to the same cell in the prison we went. I was exhausted and anxious, but still a little bit hopeful. I did not dare to talk with any of the others. Later that evening a guard came for me and took me to the office where someone told me the court had decided to release me.

'They gave me my clothes, I signed for my old trousers and shirt then I was ready to leave. I could tell the guards were wondering how I had managed this, because so few prisoners ever walked out of the gates. I asked them for my little address book so I could call someone to come and get me because I did not dare to be out in the evening, breaking the curfew. It would have been too cruel to be arrested just outside the prison! From the guard's desk, I dialled Kumara's number. He answered at once.

'I said, "Kumara, I have been released from prison. I'm sorry to trouble you but please can you come and get me? I have no other way of getting home."'

'Para my friend, it's no trouble. I am already here, waiting by the prison gates. Just come outside.'

'It was so good to hear his friendly voice!

'So I made my way through the gates and there they all were with a van—Jayantha and Abi, Kumara and his wife, son and brother … and my cousin. He had a dark face, he was still very cross with me for causing all this trouble, but I could tell he was also very pleased and relieved to see me freed.'

17

COLOMBO TO CHENNAI

Now he was released, Para just wanted to go home to shower and to recover, but his cousin said, 'Let's all go to a restaurant', so off they went.

'While we ate, my cousin told us that we had to leave Colombo and Sri Lanka as soon as possible,' Para says. 'We could choose to travel to Malaysia or to India—it was easiest to get visas for those two countries. Jayantha at once chose India because it was closer to Sri Lanka—we still hoped to return when the war ended.

'So we finished dinner and returned to our house, and gave my cousin our birth certificates and other documents. He told me to stay in the house, but we should prepare to move out within a week. "I'm telling you, Para, do not leave this house, not for anything. Just stay inside. If there is a round-up and they come for you, too many people will be in danger because so many people have done a lot to help you. I'm telling you again, stay inside."

'I was only too happy to oblige—I was still in agony from

the beatings and the "treatment" and I was terrified they may come for me again.'

After his cousin left, Para asked Kumara to explain how they had managed to organise his release.

The next day Kumara went with Jayantha and Abi to the passport office with Para's papers. Within eight days they had organised flights and visas to India.

'The only problem was what to do with all our household things—the stove, the gas, everything we had bought for Abi after he was born,' Para says. 'Once again we had to decide to just leave everything behind and give it to Kumara. We also had to pay the bond to the house owner, and we asked him to pay the money to Kumara once he found another tenant. Kumara had done so much, it was good to be able to repay him a little.

'You could follow our lives if you followed the trails of household goods and bonds we left behind ourselves, but there was nothing else that we could do. If we had known that we would be fleeing several more times, we might not have been so accepting. As always, Jayantha had carefully packed her wedding sari!'

In a few days, everything was organised, and Para's cousin arrived in a van to take them to the airport. This was going to be another frightening time—they still had to leave the country, and the immigration officers were quick to suspect anyone.

'Here's the plan,' said his cousin. 'You are flying Air India so when you get to the airport you must go to a particular counter where one of the officers will be expecting you.'

He pulled out his phone and showed Para the photo. 'You must make sure that you go only to him as the others may cause trouble. If anyone suspects anything and they call CID, you are gone, and all the people who helped you will be in great danger.'

Para was shaking with fear, so his cousin pushed him aside and showed the photo to Jayantha. 'You go in front, Jayantha, and do the talking. Give Abi to Para so he can look like he is just focusing on the baby. Now here is some money in American dollars because you will need cash to get yourselves started in India. When you reach Chennai, tell the immigration staff that you are entering as tourists to visit the temples. If they ask you to prove that, show them the money, so they will think you are just taking a holiday there. I don't know when I will see you again so take care, and please, Para, I beg you to try to keep out of trouble.'

Then they all said their goodbyes. 'Dear Kumara and his wife Nilu—what good friends they had become,' Para says, 'and my cousin, so strict and so cross with me, but such a good man. A lifesaver.

'And so Jayantha and I walked into the airport, trying desperately to look unconcerned, like two teachers and their baby going for a holiday in India, while all the time our hearts were thumping and I was concentrating on moving normally—which was still almost impossible, given my injuries. Poor Abi, I was trying so hard to keep calm that I think I squeezed him really tightly, but luckily he did not complain.'

They found the queue, and Jayantha recognised the man whose counter they needed to go to.

'He looked up at one point, and we exchanged glances,' Para says. 'I wondered if he was also anxious. We tried to appear casual, talking about anything that came into our heads, and endeavouring to look relaxed.

'Then finally it was our turn—but oh no, the queue had moved faster than we thought, and the wrong man was waving us forwards! "Quickly," muttered Jayantha, "put Abi on the floor." So I did, somehow managing not to drop him, and Jayantha fiddled with his clothes, and smiled nicely at the people behind us and told them to take our place. She pulled Abi's clothes straight, keeping one eye on "our" man and the second he was free she whipped up Abi, pushed him into my arms and set off with the bags. I was sweating and dizzy but managed to just keep up with her and talk softly to Abi.

'The man at the counter took our three passports then he looked directly at me and said, "How is your cousin?" I was so surprised, but I just told him my cousin was fine, and he was in the airport somewhere. Then, just as I thought I would die from suspense, he shuffled our passports together, handed them to Jayantha and wished us a good flight.'

The little family had an agonising wait in the departures lounge before they were finally called to board the flight with the other passengers to India.

'Slowly, so slowly, we lined up and followed the other passengers past the airline staff who were taking the boarding passes. I thought my heart would thump right out of my chest—I was surprised no one else seemed to hear it. A woman stopped me for a moment. I nearly fainted on the spot but she just wanted to smile at Abi in my arms. I felt like sprinting to the plane. It was lucky my injuries prevented that. I had to concentrate on looking calm, looking forward, never looking back, holding my son. Then we were on the plane, in our seats.'

As the plane roared down the runway, Para and Jayantha clasped hands, looked at each other and, for the first time in many weeks, smiled.

* * *

Para's first impressions of Chennai were good.

'As the plane came into land, we looked out of the windows and saw it was a dry and dusty place—very much like the Vanni area back in Sri Lanka, which is not much of a recommendation as the Vanni was desolate and destroyed by the long war. But in the airport, we immediately noticed the familiar language—Tamil signs were everywhere, and people were speaking in Tamil. The airport staff were wearing traditional Tamil clothes and we began to feel safe.'

Jayantha was also delighted. 'I thought we Tamils had nowhere to go, certainly not Tamil Eelam in the north of Sri Lanka. That was a dream destroyed. But there we were in Tamil Nadu; we soon registered with the Foreigner Regional Registration Office—the FRRO—and it felt like we could belong here.'

They were pleased to be met by Kalai, another of Para's cousins who had left Sri Lanka a few years beforehand and was studying hotel management in Chennai. He took them to his flat and they sank, exhausted, into his chairs.

'What's the plan?' he asked.

The events of the last month descended on them like a wake of vultures. The arrest, the torture, the imprisonment, the trial, the weeks of terror and uncertainty … Para looked at Jayantha and saw how tired and drawn she was. How could he have let it come to this? He could barely walk, he would have to undergo weeks of treatment to repair his body, and at that moment he doubted if he would ever repair his mind. He sighed.

'There is no plan. Not today.'

Just then, little Abi turned and smiled at the anxious adults. He did not know about terror and torture, fear and pain, doubt and uncertainty—as long as his 'Amma' and 'Appi' were there, he was happy. Para smiled back at his son, his resolve returning.

'But we'll have a plan by tomorrow,' he said.

Kalai was friendly with the house owner—his landlord—and he arranged for Jayantha and Para to rent a room in the house for one month. But the rent was high and without jobs they were rapidly using up their savings. Jayantha was pawning all the jewellery Para had given her, so soon they would have nothing. It was time to find cheaper accommodation.

Kalai had a motorbike so each day, as soon as he arrived home from his studies, he and Para would set off, hunting for somewhere to rent. Even though Para was in constant, searing pain from the torture, they had to find somewhere to live, and without delay.

Wherever they enquired, house owners would turn them away because they were Sri Lankan Tamils. With the war still raging and the thousands of Tamils flooding in from Sri Lanka, many Indians thought they would bring trouble, so they preferred not to rent to them.

Finally, good news. They found a small house they could afford to rent in Pozhichaloor, and moved in quickly. The owners were from another Indian state—Kerala—but they spoke Tamil and had two nice children.

Now they had a home, Para could attend to his injuries. At Tambaram Private Hospital Para was examined by a sympathetic doctor and given a quote for the surgery he needed.

'Forty thousand rupees; eight hundred dollars,' he says. 'A crazy sum for us, but we just had to go ahead. Kalai was great; he loaned us most of the money. And Jayantha pawned more of her jewels. She had very little left now, just a few bracelets and necklaces. This is how we managed—in good times I would buy her jewellery, then in bad times she would pawn pieces so we had enough money to live. I hated seeing her go to the pawnshop, but right then, there was nothing I could do.'

After the operation, Para was sent home to rest, with a nurse coming twice each day to dress the wounds. The nurse also needed paying, which meant more trips to the pawnshop. 'When I bought the bracelets for Jayantha, I never imagined how useful they would be in the future.'

It took a month to heal. Jayantha cared for Para and Abi, as well as taking over all the household chores.

Jayantha was unhappy at first. 'People were not friendly towards her, and many words in their Tamil were different from ours. When she went shopping, there were numerous things she couldn't ask for—necessities like flour and so on—and the shopkeepers were rude, telling her to stand aside if she couldn't explain what she wanted.'

But Jayantha refused to give up and asked the house owner to tell her the names of everything. Soon she was managing perfectly.

Money remained a daily concern, but Para's brother and sister helped them at this time, sending money until Para recovered enough to work. But what could he do? Jobs were almost impossible to obtain, as so many Tamils had streamed in from Sri Lanka.

Then Jayantha had an idea. 'In our area were thousands of Sri Lanka Tamil boys, living in cramped rooms with no way of cooking for themselves—no facilities and no space. But many were doing heavy manual jobs, so they needed food for their lunches to keep them going. No one had a wife or mother to cook—they had all fled to India from the fighting, leaving their families behind, and now they needed someone to feed them.' So Para went from house to house with Abi on his shoulders, asking if anyone needed lunches.

A routine quickly developed. 'I would get up at 4 a.m., leaving Jayantha sleeping with Abi, and put the rice in the cooker, break open and scrape the coconuts, chop the onions and slice the chillies. Then I would waken Jayantha and look after Abi while she cooked huge pots of curry. While the food cooled, we would open up all the containers and then pack the food—eighteen rupees per person for four curries, one fry and one rice. We put the rice in small containers and the curries in bags. I put all the parcels into a big box and was then ready to deliver to the bus stop on the old motorbike we had bought for eight thousand rupees [$160 Australian dollars]. It was old and battered, had no mirrors and really roared, but it never let us down. I used to balance the big box on the fuel tank.

'Wherever I went, Abi wanted to come too, but of course he couldn't fit on the bike when I had the food. So every morning I would tell him I was going to get something from the bedroom, and he would wait outside the door. Then I would quickly tiptoe round and out through the other door, without him seeing me. Then I would push the bike quietly away, and start it up when I was some distance from the house, so he wouldn't hear me.'

After he delivered the food parcels, Para would return and take Abi for his ride.

'We started so early each day that we worried that the house owners would grow tired from the noise, but they were wonderful—sometimes we slept late because we were so tired, and then they would call up the stairs to waken us.'

After the deliveries, they had to go to the markets to buy the vegetables. By going later, they managed to buy food more cheaply. 'Jayantha and Abi did not like the fish market—it smelled terribly—but Jayantha said I was a hopeless negotiator and insisted on going there until she found a nice woman to bargain with for the best prices. After that, I was allowed to go alone.

'We had no fridge or freezer, so everything was always fresh, and we varied the menu to have two vegetarian dishes each week. It worked well until the power supply went off, then we would have to cook everything on the gas, which meant we were late getting to the bus stop, the boys had already set off to their jobs, and I had to deliver the food parcels to where the boys were working. It was so far away that we lost everything in fuel costs. Power cuts were really bad for us.

'Although the food business started well, after a while the boys found they needed to save more money to send back to their families, so they stopped buying food from us. They preferred Jayantha's cooking to the rice and soup they bought, but for that they paid only two rupees each day. So it was time for me to get another job while Jayantha continued with our catering business.'

Para's new job involved working for Jeeva, another cousin recently arrived in Chennai. Jeeva fled to India after his brother was arrested and murdered by the Sri Lanka Army.

'He was arrested and he disappeared. Then a few weeks later dogs found his body decomposing in the jungle. Jeeva was very scared and thought he should run away before the soldiers came for him.'

Jeeva had established a small painting business, and he was happy to give Para a job. Although he was a good painter, Jeeva was not a successful businessman, but with Para's organisational skills the business soon developed.

'I noticed that a few of the men were stealing brushes and some paint, so I helped Jeeva to organise some systems. Then I realised that some men were paid more than others. Jeeva told me this was like "danger money" paid to the painters who went up on the outsides of buildings, suspended on a sort of cradle—two ropes with a plank in the middle. Since I needed all the money I could earn, I asked to do this job. It was very scary—if it was windy the plank would swing and the bucket of paint would slide, tilting the cradle at crazy angles. I started at the top of the building, then each time I finished a section, I had to whistle to the boy up on the roof and ask him to lower the plank. Once we had started a job, we had to finish it quickly before the paint changed colour in the hot sunshine.

'It was hot, hard and dangerous work, but it was a job, I was getting paid and we were managing. I was very grateful to Jeeva for giving me the opportunity to work.'

Once again, though, events beyond his control were about to send Para off on another 'adventure'.

At the time, there were one hundred and thirty-two camps housing five hundred thousand refugees from Sri Lanka, and many ex-LTTE soldiers were coming in from the war zones. They didn't want to fight any more—many of them had been forcibly conscripted, anyway. Everyone was told to register with the police when they arrived, but many did not, so the Indian Intelligence Service would go around the houses at night and round up all the Sri Lankan Tamils they could find. If they did not have registration, then they were arrested and handed over to the Sri Lankan forces.

'Obviously, we didn't want this to happen—imagine if they came across me again!' Para says. 'So we decided I should leave Chennai for a while to avoid any trouble. But where to go?'

Cousin Kalai came to the rescue—through his contacts in the hospitality industry, he knew of a hotel in Nepal. Before he knew it, Para found himself with a few other Tamils on a two-day train ride to Kolkata, then crossing the border into Nepal.

'I didn't know the first thing about Nepalese food, so I had to learn everything from A to Z in a hurry. I started off washing dishes. We lived in a bunkroom—eight of us in four beds on either side of the room, all squashed so tightly so you could not even sit up. We had to get up very early each morning and pack up our things to leave the room clean. It was hard work, but I didn't have to buy food—we ate the scraps and leftovers—so I was able to go to the Western Union Bank on my day off and send money to Jayantha. I tried to call her every day, and she was managing, but again, it was not the life I wanted for her and Abi.'

After about eight months Jayantha told Para that things seemed quieter in Chennai and it would be okay for him to return, so he finished up in the restaurant and went back to see them. 'I had missed them terribly, and Abi had grown so much. I thought, I really don't want to be ever separated from them again.'

But once back in Chennai, Para and Jayantha came to realise how impossible their situation was.

'We had come to Chennai on three-month tourist visas, yet by now we had stayed for two years. I could have been asked to present my visa at any time, and would have been arrested on the spot when the police saw the dates. All around us Sri Lankan Tamils were in the same position, with people still being returned.'

It was late 2009 and by now the war had ended, with Mahinda Rajapaksa's government in power. The Tamils had been slaughtered in their thousands, and even though the government had completely destroyed the LTTE, along with any possibility of a separate state, they were frightened of a resistance movement growing, so they continued terrifying Tamils with round-ups and the notorious white vans, imprisonment and torture. Many thousands of people were missing—taken by the police or army, so returning to Sri Lanka was not an option.

'But in India, life was also complicated. We were not Indians, so we were not allowed to own a business or a property. We were expected to register—but registration would have meant being caught without the correct visa. We made a little money selling food, but even that was dangerous because we could not register the business. The refugee camps were terrible, and outside the camps tensions were rising between the local population and refugees. Attacks were widespread, with refugees blamed for everything, including the sudden increase in the price of consumer goods and rents.

'We could not see a future for ourselves or Abi—we felt Sri Lankan Tamils were definitely no longer welcome in India.'

18
THE DECISION IS MADE

At this point, Para's cousin came to Chennai to see how they were getting on.

Tamils were leaving India as fast as they could, heading to any country that would take them, but the airports were watched, and many people were arrested as they tried to leave. Switzerland, Germany, Canada and the UK—Tamils were willing to go anywhere to distance themselves from their country of birth. The government was ignoring calls to account for its terrible human rights record, and people were still being rounded up. It was a dark time—every young Tamil man was suspected of working for the LTTE, people were trying to recover from nearly thirty years of civil war, and families were still separated, not knowing what had happened to loved ones.

'We talked with my cousin for a long time. We knew that for me to return to Sri Lanka would be terribly dangerous, after my work as student president. Then there were the records of my arrests and imprisonment—I had never done anything criminal, but the police would definitely have my name on their files. And that alone was enough to have me arrested again.

'We discussed everything from every angle then finally my cousin told me that he thought I had only one option—to travel by boat to another country, and ask for asylum when I arrived. "It will be quite safe," he said. "A few days at sea, then when you arrive in Australia you can send for Jayantha and Abi."

'I shake my head and smile when I think about that conversation. My cousin was a good man; he helped me so much—and my brother and sister, and all my other cousins. But his information on travelling to Australia by boat to seek asylum was not quite accurate. Of course, in Chennai in 2009 I had no way of knowing the reality of the situation for people seeking asylum in Australia. In hindsight, that was probably a good thing.

'I told him we would think about what he had said. "Well, think quickly," he replied. "Time is not on your side."'

After his cousin left them, Jayantha and Para clung together, two-year-old Abi pressed between them. Once again, their lives had reached a crossroads. Acting on limited information, working on borrowed time, they needed to take a momentous decision that would affect the rest of their lives.

'We all have choices, and throughout our lives we have to decide what to do,' Para says. 'I always wanted to make the right choice, but in those awful, extraordinary times, it was often impossible to know which was the right way.

'I was thinking—already when I was just a teenager I'd had to choose whether to study hard and try for university, or decide to stay with my family and be content with being a farmer.

'Then at university I had to choose whether to accept the nomination for student leader, to lead the students and negotiate with the LTTE and the army, or to just study quietly and become a teacher.

'Before I asked Jayantha to marry me, I had to think about the consequences of that—we knew we would be shunned by both our families for marrying out of caste; could I impose that on her? In such dangerous times, death was constantly stalking us—what if I was killed? Would I waste her life? And what about Abi—should we have decided to have a baby, given the war and all the problems? That was a massive decision. But we chose to marry and to have a baby.

'And why move from Mannar when we both had good jobs as teachers? Should we have stayed, hoping there would not be another round-up, hoping I would not be arrested, hoping the war would somehow not affect us? Weighing the risks, we chose to move.

'Then, should I have stayed working in Trincomalee, just hoping for the best, or was it the right decision to leave quickly before Karuna soldiers came for me? And in Colombo, after the torture and prison, should I have left Sri Lanka, or would it have been better to hide away somewhere? Once again, those decisions were relatively straightforward— we knew what was happening to thousands of Tamils who were arrested at that time; the army would have kept coming for me, we had to keep moving.

'Now here was another "choice"—should I leave my wife and son, in the hope of finally finding safety for us all, or should I stay? Should I get onto a flimsy boat and place my life in the hands of strangers, hoping one of them could find the way to Australia across a gigantic ocean, or should I just hope we could make a life in Chennai, avoiding immigration officials for the rest of time?'

Those had been Para's choices. Should he have risked everything, trying to find a better life for his wife and son—one where they could live in peace, not fearing the sound of a white van engine, the barking dogs, the boots in the lane, the knock at the door, the glance in the street? Should he have stayed with them in India? The possibility of forced repatriation to Sri Lanka was extremely high; every day, people were being returned from India, and facing horrific consequences.

Whatever the dangers of the high seas, Para and Jayantha thought the risks of remaining in Chennai were higher. Stay or go? Stay or go?

'I chose to go. This time I was risking everything.'

Travelling by boat to Australia to seek asylum was a dangerous and extreme solution, but Para and Jayantha felt this was their only chance to find a peaceful life together with their baby son.

They knew the voyage would be risky and that the next few weeks would be filled with uncertainty and danger, but returning to Sri Lanka was simply not an option. The war may have ended, but every day reports were coming out of Sri Lanka that Tamils were still being kidnapped by government security forces, thrown in the back of white vans, and never seen again.

'The civil war in Sri Lanka had already caused so much heartache and disruption, and taken so many innocent lives,'

The decision is made

Para says. 'Families had been destroyed or ripped apart, brothers, sisters and cousins had separated from their parents and were living in different continents. At least, the luckier ones were. Many of those who had not managed to escape were now incarcerated in secret prisons in the north, or were perpetually on the move, trying to avoid the aftermath of such a cruel and bloody war. My own family had been badly affected, with so many aunts, uncles, cousins and friends maimed and killed. No one emerged unscathed from the war, and the aftershocks continued, with constant reports of disappearances and murders.

'In India we were faced with the constant threat of deportation, and we had heard what happened to people who were returned to Sri Lanka. We knew we couldn't stay.

'My plan was to sail to Australia, to ask for asylum and then to find a job and save some money so I could send for Jayantha and Abi.

'It was a plan. Not a perfect plan, as it turned out, but it was all we had at the time.'

Around the Tamils' haunts in Chennai there were whispers of two boats preparing to make the dangerous journey to Australia. Para was keen to put his name on the list. But first, he was told he had to find twelve thousand American dollars. This sum was simply beyond the reach of a young man who in the last two years had earned just a few rupees each day, painting the outsides of buildings and washing dishes in a Nepalese kitchen. The only solution was to borrow the money. Para hated asking his family and friends for help yet again, but the need to escape drove him to call his brother Panneer in England and sister Pugalini in Switzerland.

'I called them both and each of them said they would help me. If they had not sent money, then I would have been in terrible trouble, stuck in Chennai with no way out. My brother and my sister saved my life, again. I will never forget it.'

The problem now was finding a way to collect the cash his brother and sister sent. The money was transferred to Western Union, and could only be collected by people holding Indian identity cards. But Sri Lankan nationals living in India did not have these. Finally, Para persuaded his landlord to collect the money on his behalf. One thousand American dollars was to be paid in advance, with the remaining eleven thousand to be handed over once he reached his destination.

'Then I went with some of the boys from my painting job to meet a man in a small shop in Chennai and showed him the money. He told me to prepare to leave, and that I would be contacted by phone when it was time.'

Jayantha and Para both believed that it would be possible for him to reach Australia by boat, and that once Para was there, he could find work and then send for his wife and son. They knew the risks, but felt they had no choice.

As the time to depart drew near, Jayantha asked, 'Before you go, can we organise Abi's Vidyarambam?' During this traditional ceremony, parents take their child to the temple and help them to write the first letter of the alphabet on a bed of rice. This usually marks the beginning of formal education, with the child around five or six years old.

'Abi was only two years old, but Jayantha was worried it might be a long time before we were together again,' Para says, 'and she wanted us to do this so she could start teaching Abi in my absence.

'We could not afford to have our ceremony at the temple, so instead Jayantha made a special area in our home. We were living in just one small room, with a shower and a kitchen, but Jayantha decorated it with pictures of the gods, and fruit and flowers, and she prepared a plate of rice. Abi thought something exciting was happening—he was too young to understand what was going on, and he had no idea I was going to be leaving him. Jayantha prepared our *pooja* [made the space ready for the ritual], and we prayed and marked our foreheads in the customary way.

'Just as we were holding his tiny hands, helping him to trace the letters in the rice, my phone started ringing. Jayantha and I looked at each other—we knew it would be the agent. My heart beat faster but I ignored the phone and just kept holding Abi, helping him to trace the letters.'

Then Para's phone rang again, and this time Jayantha answered it. 'The agent said, "It's time for Para to go by train to Mangalore. Tell him to go quickly." Jayantha just looked at me with tears in her eyes and Abi stared at us both, sensing something was wrong.

"Please let us come to the train station with you," Jayantha murmured. I picked up the small bag that Jayantha had packed for me, then we went into the street and hired an auto to take us to the station. On the way, we stopped at the temple and prayed to Shiva, then we continued to the station. When we had nearly arrived I told Jayantha that I knew Abi would be too sad to let me go on the train, so it would be better that she returned home there and then, to avoid him getting upset in the crowded station.

'I held them tightly one last time, then we parted. Abi was crying and crying, and I didn't dare to look at him because my heart was breaking too.

'Abi was just two years old. I had bought him a baby doll. He still has that doll and always keeps it close. Even now I feel the pain of that leaving. I had only ever wanted to look after Jayantha, and to make her proud of me. When Abi was born, I thought my heart would burst with love and happiness. But here I was—there we were—saying goodbye near a crowded station, not knowing if we would ever see each other again. I was not afraid for myself, I was afraid for Jayantha and Abi—how could I leave them? But then how could I stay? Leaving them was the worst thing I've ever had to do in my life and I hope no one else is ever faced with such a dilemma.'

One last glimpse of his wife and son, and they had gone. Para pushed his way into the station, bought his ticket then squeezed aboard the train, surrounded by thousands, yet isolated in grief. The train journey passed in a blur; he did not notice the usual chaos, the pushing and squashing, the shouting and the general cacophony that is travel in India.

Para had been ordered to make his way by train from Chennai to the fishing port of Mangalore, and wait there quietly, without drawing attention to himself, for further directives.

Arriving in Mangalore, Para followed instructions and made his way to the small hotel, where he found a few Tamil men already waiting. Squeezed in, six or seven to the room, they slept on mats and spoke quietly and anxiously among themselves, taking care to avoid making contact with other groups of Tamils around the port.

The decision is made

After a few days a man came, masked to conceal his identity. He greeted the anxious men, saying, 'We're going to send you all to Australia. We have two fishing boats to take you from the port here to international waters, then we'll transfer you to a big ship. You can bring only one change of clothes and a small packet of documents. Nothing else. Wait here and we'll call for you in two to three days.'

The men waited in the stifling room for one more day, hardly daring to talk among themselves, not knowing who could be trusted, even there.

Then night came. Someone in heavy disguise arrived and instructed everyone to quickly leave the hotel and get into the buses waiting outside.

Nervously, they slipped out of the hotel and into the battered old buses that groaned their way towards the harbour and then parked in the shadows some distance from the wharves. It was dark and hot. Nobody spoke and nothing happened. The men waited anxiously, sweating in the heat of the night, poised to move but managing to remain still.

Suddenly the buses turned and headed back to the hotel, where everyone was told to quickly disembark and return to their rooms. Nerves jangled as they anticipated further instructions. What had happened? Would they be able to get away? Men who had lived with such fear for so long were finding it hard to keep themselves from panicking.

However, they managed somehow to keep each other calm, and at two thirty the following morning the agent returned, demanding haste, stealth and silence.

19
THE JOURNEY

Quickly and quietly, Para and the others once more slipped out of the hotel, squeezed into another small bus that was already crammed with frightened young men, and drove back down to the harbour. Peering through the grimy windows, Para saw that alongside the dock were two boats, one large and heavy, and the other ramshackle, rusted and tiny.

'Quickly, move quickly,' were the whispered instructions as groups of ten were ordered off the buses and ushered along the wharf. Para estimated around one hundred and twenty to one hundred and thirty people were hurriedly embarked onto the bigger boat on that hot, dark night. When he was allowed off his bus he was pushed towards the small boat, with no chance to swap, as the bigger boat had already slipped its moorings and moved away from the dock, engines thrumming gently. Soon it was just a blur in the night.

Para was horrified at the sight of the smaller boat, grating and groaning alongside the dock, bobbing on the swell made by the larger vessel. The sides were warped and peeling, the tiny cabin looked as if it only balanced on the splintered decks, and the whole boat seemed almost too old to float, let alone sail away. A few men started to complain that the boat was not seaworthy, but they were told they would transfer to a bigger ship once they were in international waters. And if they didn't like it, they could leave. Refunds were not mentioned.

The men held back, frightened to climb on such a battered little boat. Then a hissed instruction: 'Stop talking. Quickly, get on board and hide yourselves below. We're leaving now.'

Para and the remaining men and boys hastily jumped down onto the ancient deck and scrambled into the steaming and stinking engine room below, where they were almost overcome with diesel fuel fumes and smells from rotten fish and they didn't know what else. Vomiting and gasping, they immediately tried to clamber out, but they were ordered to stay below, hidden from view.

It took only minutes for the little boat to sail, with three crew on top and about thirty-six people hiding below.

After several hours, they were allowed to creep out of the hold, one by one, and ordered to hide around the deck, keeping their heads down out of sight. Viewed from another craft, the little boat would have appeared to be a simple fishing vessel, with a normal crew of four men.

The precautions of the crew were justified when a large Indian naval boat approached suddenly through the dark waters, came alongside, and asked the captain what he was doing.

'You are not fishing—the waters here are too deep for that. You should go back towards land.'

The Power of Good People

Would they be sent back before they had made any progress? The Tamils lay quietly in their hiding places, heads down, avoiding detection. They must have been spotted, but their captain gave some money to the naval boat and it pulled away, leaving them all shaken by the close encounter and relieved to be going forward.

For a few hours, the little boat chugged on. Apart from the white gleam of the waves breaking at its bow, caught in the silvery light of the moon, everything was dark. Each man was sitting tensely, alarmed by their close encounter, longing for the meeting with the bigger ship when—they had been told—they would climb on board and set sail for freedom.

Para had a chance now to look at the crew. The captain, from India, was only around twenty-five years old, and was accompanied by two boys aged around fifteen and sixteen, and one man around thirty. No one apart from the crew was allowed in the cabin, and there did not appear to be any maps or equipment.

Para was not overly concerned by this—he was sure everything would be stowed neatly, waiting for them on the bigger ship. 'We were told the other ship had food, water, oil, gas and lifejackets. We believed them. What else could we do?'

This little boat might have been decrepit and with hardly any supplies, but Para kept telling himself it was just like a water taxi, taking them safely from the dock to transfer at sea to the bigger vessel. Or so he hoped.

'For four days we sailed, but we didn't move very far, we just waited,' he says. 'This was not what we had expected, but we had to put up with it. Every day we hoped the big boat would arrive. We were not allowed to cook in case a Sri Lankan naval vessel saw the flames or smoke; we just ate biscuits and some dried fruits. We had to mostly hide in the engine room below, but at night we were allowed to come on the deck as long as we kept down, kept quiet, kept everything dark and didn't smoke. We also had to move carefully so we didn't upset the balance.'

Their journey was now taking them close to Sri Lankan shores, and they were worried they might be intercepted by the Sri Lankan navy—that would definitely have ended badly. They had all heard terrible stories about treatment of Tamils who were caught trying to escape. The wrath of the Rajapaksa government knew no bounds—having won the war, it did not choose to show compassion in peace.

Para did not ask anyone about their personal circumstances. There would be plenty of time for talking later; for now, it was enough to know that each man on that boat had a reason for taking such a risk to flee the country of their birth. Maybe they were suspected of being involved—willingly or unwillingly—with the Tamil Tigers, so were clear targets for the government forces as they went around the country, 'mopping up'.

Maybe they had nothing to stay for, having lost everyone they knew and loved. Many families were wiped out in a single bomb blast—the small shelters they dug and covered with branches and coconut leaves offered little protection when civilians were directly targeted. And many people who had survived the constant shelling succumbed later to sickness or starvation. Often the only option was to leave and try to start over in a new country.

Whatever their reasons for fleeing, each man must have felt this was the only solution—to leave all that he once had and loved, in the hope of finding sanctuary. Those like Para, with wives and children, hoped they would soon be able to bring them to a new home where there was no war, no kidnapping, torture, rape and murder, and where they could work hard, contribute to their new country, and live happily ever after. Sadly, as time would tell, 'happily ever after' is the language of fairy tales.

But Para did not know this then—he just hoped this venture would turn out well as he lay on the ropes, feeling ill, lulled by the vibrations of the motor and worrying about Jayantha and Abi.

'We were divided into two groups, with one group sitting at the front of the boat and the other at the back,' he says. 'I was told to sit at the back of the boat with a chubby man. At first I just smiled at him, but after a few days we started talking and he told me his name was Sinnathambi. Like me, he had left behind his wife, and she was living in Chennai with their daughter. He had been a mechanic in Sri Lanka but had to leave because he had worked on vehicles belonging to the LTTE. It did not matter to the army that the LTTE soldiers would have shot him if he'd refused.'

The boat was so small that they had to be careful to keep it balanced, so more men sat at the front to keep the boat going straight through the waves. Sometimes a rogue wave would violently rock the boat, causing everyone to roll across to one side, then the crew would shout at them to get back to their positions quickly, to set the boat straight again. Para only weighed about fifty kilograms so he was easily thrown around the deck, but he learned he could hold onto the bigger and heavier Sinnathambi.

'It was very hard to use the toilet,' Para says. 'The crew had cut a hole in the deck at the back of the boat, so we could squat there over the open water. An old sarong was nailed up to give some privacy, but it was very hard to keep our dignity, especially when the boat rocked. And we had to be very careful to remember to replace the lid, or water would have flooded up and onto the deck.'

On the fifth day, they were finally allowed to cook. 'There was only rice provided because we were waiting to meet the big boat with the supplies. The stove was sliding around the deck, so we tied it down alongside the gas cylinder. At first two men held onto the pot, but the boiling water gave some serious burns, so some men found lengths of wire in the engine room and used it to tie the handles of the pot to two posts to keep it steady. It worked, but someone still needed to hold onto the lid. It was a lot of effort for a small bowl of rice. As well, we only had about ten soft plastic dishes between us, and these folded up when we put the hot rice on them, so it was nearly impossible to eat the *kanchi*.[1]

'One of the crew caught some fish using a rope and cooked it on the stove. It smelt terrible but they told us to eat it anyway, to keep up our energy, and that fishermen ate it when they were at sea. Sometimes we were allowed to boil water and put teabags in the pot to make tea. There was only one two-kilo bag of sugar, so everyone had just one teaspoon.

---

1 Rice porridge made by boiling rice and water until it's the consistency of porridge.

There were only two mugs so it took a long time for nearly forty people to get a drink.'

After a few days, the men were getting restless. With no land in sight, it was hard to tell if the little boat was making any progress. Para felt it was not really moving.

'People were getting frustrated. They started asking the crew about the big boat—where was it? Where were all the supplies? The crew said nothing, but I thought they looked anxious. I began to wonder if everything was all right.'

Still no one was allowed in the cabin, but they could hear the crackling static of the radio, so they assumed everything was still going to plan. The fifth night passed slowly, but the men stayed hopeful, expecting to see the big ship at any time.

Finally, when pink streaks on the horizon heralded the sixth day, the crew seemed extremely preoccupied. Something was wrong.

The captain came down to speak to them.

'I have terrible news,' he said. 'The other big boat isn't coming. We were talking with their crew over the radio when they told us they had been spotted by the Sri Lankan navy, and then there was an explosion and we have not heard from them again. We believe they were attacked and have sunk.'

Everyone was appalled. Many people on Para's boat had friends and relatives on the bigger vessel.

'People were shocked and crying,' Para recalls. 'We felt hopeless and frightened. We had all heard that the Sri Lankan navy was sinking boats full of escaping Tamils, but we hadn't really believed it. Which country sinks a boat full of its own people? Now we knew. I thanked the gods that

The journey

I was not on the other ship—what would Jayantha and Abi do without me?'

When one of the men asked the captain, 'What about us? What are we going to do now?', they were told there were two options.

'We can go back to where we started from, and this will take us another six days. When we arrive, we will all be arrested by the Indian Navy. Everyone will be put in prison and most of you will be deported to Sri Lanka. Or, we can go on and try to reach Australia in this boat.'

It was a dilemma.

'How long will it take us to get to Australia?' Para asked. 'This boat is so old and battered; can it actually make the journey?'

The captain replied he didn't know how long it would take, because it all depended on the weather. And the question of whether the boat would last that long could only be answered by the gods.

In the end, everyone decided to go on, but then they were told they had to wait a few more days for supplies to come from Colombo.

'Colombo?' Para says. 'We were very scared to think we were close to Colombo, but the captain told us we were in international waters, so we should be safe. We agreed to wait for the supplies—we had no choice. For two more days we waited, wondered and grieved for our friends on the bigger boat.'

Everyone was quiet; many prayed and no one smiled. They all thought their lives would be over in a day or so. Fortunately, the sea was calm and the men were allowed to go in for a much needed swim to wash themselves and their filthy clothes. Many jumped straight into the ocean but Para, a non-swimmer, had to hold onto a rope.

'I was scared about the sharks, but Sinnathambi told me he had seen dolphins and this meant there were no sharks around. I now know that's not true, but I believed it then and it gave me the confidence to go in, holding tightly to a rope. Then suddenly I saw someone in trouble, and splashing and calling for help. One of the crew swam out and rescued him. I started noticing which of the men were strong swimmers—I thought I should make sure I was friends with them, so I'd be prepared if this old boat sank!'

From that day, they saw many dolphins. 'They came alongside the boat with their beautiful smiling faces, and were friendly and inquisitive. The people who were sitting at the sides of the boat could reach out and touch them. I felt that our luck was improving—it was hard to be gloomy alongside a pod of dolphins. And then we started seeing schools of flying fish—they were beautiful, flashes of silver and blue, launching themselves out of the ocean. Sometimes they landed on the deck and we carefully picked them up and put them back in the sea. I wanted to fly like those fish until someone told me they fly out of the ocean to escape from predators. Then I knew how they felt.'

On the eighth day, they saw a Sri Lankan fishing boat in the distance, heading towards them.

'We quickly hid in the engine room, taking care to keep the boat balanced. The fishing boat came alongside and the Sinhalese fishermen on board asked our crew for cigarettes, then sailed away. They could have seen us hiding and we were worried they might tell the Sri Lankan navy about us, so our captain decided to move away from the area and keep our boat in darkness.

'Just before sunset we could see a navy boat in the far distance which seemed to be searching for us. We were told to keep quiet and not to smoke. We were all very scared because now we knew what would happen if they saw us. Eventually, we saw the lights of the big navy boat heading away, but our captain decided to keep moving and make a different meeting place in case the navy came back to look for us in daylight.

'We picked up speed, and seemed to have gone a long way, when we heard our crew speaking on the radio in Sinhala and around 6 p.m., we saw a boat coming towards us. When it arrived their crew told us to transfer things very quickly so we helped to take on rice, sugar, noodles, coconuts, dates, oils, gas, biscuits, tinned fish and diesel. As well, two other Tamils jumped on board—they had come directly from Sri Lanka. Then that boat quickly set off and soon vanished over the horizon. Our captain told us we had enough food for ten to fifteen days. And so we finally started off for Australia.'

Para assumed the supplies had been arranged by the agent or 'people smuggler'.

'People can be quick to condemn people smugglers and yes, many of them are bad people, taking advantage of refugees and asylum seekers. But when you really do have no other way, then people smugglers become your lifeline. The man in charge of our operation—the agent—could have left us to our fate once the other boat was sunk, but somehow he managed to arrange a delivery of supplies from Colombo to our little boat in the ocean. We were literally fleeing for our lives; without our agent, we would all probably have ended up back in Sri Lanka and been killed. At the time, no one else in the world was prepared to help us.'

On the tenth day, everyone was in better spirits and formed themselves into groups for cooking and other duties. Para and Sinnathambi made tea and washed dishes.

'After we received the supplies, people were happier, and a few were even singing and dancing because they thought we would soon be in Australia,' Para says. 'Then one of the men, who was a fisherman, told us we had only just passed Sri Lanka, and still had a very long way to go.

'So everyone went quiet again. And that night the waves were huge and the boat was rolling, and we were all sick and soaked. Sinnathambi kept checking on the engine and updating the crew. Most people were either scared or still terribly sad about their lost relatives on the other boat.'

20

THE DISASTER UNFOLDS

As the days passed, the men came to know each other's stories. They looked after each other and friendships grew. Some, like Para, were teachers, some were ex-LTTE soldiers and one, the big gentle mechanic called Sinnathambi, became a close friend.

They were all casualties of a civil war that had pervaded their country and their lives for years—in some cases, their lifetimes. Their pasts were littered with memories of dead and maimed family members caught in the crossfire of two opposing peoples. Many of the Tamils had close friends who were Sinhalese, and all of them lamented the political forces that so cruelly divided the country.

Sinnathambi was a big, strong man and Para came to rely on him to wedge him against the side of the boat as it rolled in the swell. In turn, Para frequently took over the cooking, lighting the fire and boiling water to cook the rice. With no vegetables and just a handful of spices it was hard to create anything that was little more than edible, but with no alternative the men ate it gratefully.

One day, Para noticed the youngest boy, aged about thirteen, was missing. Fearing he had fallen overboard, Para searched and found him alone in the engine room, crying softly.

'What's wrong?' he asked the dirty, dishevelled and terribly sunburned boy. 'Try not to worry, I'm sure we'll be in Australia soon.'

'I am crying because today it's my birthday,' the boy replied. 'I don't think I will see my mother again, and she will be thinking of me now and wondering where I am and what is happening to me.'

There was little Para could do to comfort the child, but later, when it was time to cook the rice, he took a little extra and scraped some coconut into it, making a small birthday cake. 'It's not much, but I hope it will make you happy for a moment,' he said. 'Let's hope that you will celebrate your next birthday in Australia.'

As it turned out, that was the boy's last birthday, ever.

By now they were far out in the Indian Ocean, and the weather was deteriorating, with massive waves tossing the boat around, and the men all succumbing to gut-wrenching seasickness. The crew told them it helped to drink seawater, which they did, to no avail. Then dark clouds gathered and the men found an old tarpaulin in the engine room and set it up to funnel rainwater into the barrels. It was oily and dirty, so the water was not pure, but they needed it badly for cooking and drinking, because their supplies had run out. The boat was bounced through the waves, sometimes across them, soaking everyone on board, but the crew seemed capable and took it in turns to steer.

The disaster unfolds

That night everyone was dozing when suddenly the boat veered sharply, throwing people around the deck. Looking up as they scrambled back to their places, they saw they had just avoided colliding with a huge cruise ship, which had not seen them because they had no lights.

After twenty or so days had passed, the food stocks were dwindling and the passengers began to wonder if everything was going to plan. One of the men finally demanded to speak with the captain and asked if he knew where they were. They were increasingly anxious, he said, and suspected that they were lost. The captain must have realised that the passengers were losing confidence. 'Just a few more days,' he told them. What could they do but hope?

Alone on the high seas with no maps and apparently no clue, the men's morale slumped further when supplies did run out. The rice porridge had seemed unappetising at the time, but now it had all gone, the men had fonder memories of their daily rations. Hunger set in and soon, as water supplies diminished, thirst.

Leaning against each other in the late afternoon, sliding around the heaving deck, Sinnathambi and Para were chatting about their hopes for the future and the mechanic's business Sinnathambi intended to establish in Australia. Suddenly Sinnathambi sat up. Something was wrong with the engine—his mechanic's ear had caught a change in the rhythm. Ignoring the crew's protests, he went below and saw the engine room was taking in water.

'We told the crew and they said this was a wooden boat, designed to cope in the ocean,' Para says. 'But the waves were massive, we were going up and down, and soon there was a different noise from the engine room and Sinnathambi said there was now so much water coming in that something must be broken. He asked for towels and shirts to plug the leak and we started baling water, but there was not much room so only two men could fit, and they passed up the buckets to others on the deck.

'Then the captain told some more men to stand at the front of the boat to stop it being swamped by the waves. Everyone was totally soaked, and we were all so cold. Then suddenly one of the men had a stroke and fell to the floor of the boat. The crew were trying to sail the boat, and we all prayed while we baled the water, kept the boat afloat and tried to look after the sick man on the floor.'

The captain finally conceded they needed to call for help, and to everyone's surprise he produced a satellite phone. The first call he made was to the head of the group that had organised the venture—the agent. He did not appear concerned about their plight, and gave the captain two numbers to call. Try the Australian Red Cross first, he suggested.

The problem now was to find someone who could speak English.

Among the thirty-nine people on the boat, it turned out that Para was the only one able and confident to make the call. The captain dialled the number and Para took the phone, silently thanking his old English teacher Subramaniyam Iyar for the hours in his classroom learning English grammar and vocabulary.

Everyone stood around Para, listening to the phone ringing. Finally, there was a connection: 'Thank you for calling the Australian Red Cross. Your call is important to us.

Unfortunately, there is no one available to take your call, so please leave a message and we will get back to you as soon as possible.'

'I am Paheer Pararasasingam,' he replied, struggling to remember his English. 'We are coming by boat to Australia, and we are sinking. Please can you send help?'

There was little more he could do, so he switched off the phone and told everyone, 'That wasn't very good. We have to wait for them to call us.'

They never did call back.

Soon the captain took the phone and called the agent again, but this time he could not get through—the agent's phone had been switched off. Everyone was aghast, but they would have been even more concerned if they had known what the agent did next.

'The agent informed all the passengers' families that the boat had sunk and all the men had died,' Para says. 'In Chennai, Jayantha was walking along the street with Abi on her way to buy groceries. Jayantha received a call from the agent and he just said, "Your husband is drowned, he died in the ocean." Then he turned off his phone so Jayantha couldn't call him back or talk to him.

'Jayantha fainted in the street, so people took her to the nearest hospital where she came around, and then she had to manage with Abi without any help. My parents were informed in Sri Lanka, and friends and family gathered at their house in sympathy.'

Jayantha tried to contact friends and families of people who may have been travelling with Para; they had all received the same news.

'Poor Jayantha could only pray at the temple,' Para says. 'Abi couldn't understand why his mum was crying, or what had happened to his dad. I am so sorry for causing such pain to Jayantha. It is another thing for which I will never forgive myself.'

On the stricken boat, prospects seemed bleak and the men were increasingly anxious as they baled the water, which was now rising around the engine. There were no lifejackets and the ocean was beginning to seem menacing.

'We have to do something else,' Sinnathambi said. 'We can't just let this boat sink from under us.'

Finally, the captain dialled the other number the agent had given him—the Australian Maritime Safety Authority (AMSA) and handed the phone to Para. The call went through to the Rescue Co-ordination Centre (RCC) located at AMSA's head office in Canberra, and was the beginning of a chain of events that would see professionalism, courage and resilience meet with indifference and selfishness as a disaster unfolded in the Indian Ocean, some five hundred nautical miles from the Cocos Islands.

* * *

The little boat that had carried them so far was now showing every sign of sinking fast. A few men were still frantically baling seawater from the engine. The others were desperate for some encouraging news.

'Everyone was gathered around me, shouting advice and questions,' Para says. 'I was scared—we all were scared. I hadn't used my English for years, and I had never spoken with a person whose first language was English. Would they understand me? I knew everyone on our boat depended on me, and I was desperately worried I would let them down. But there was no time to think it through. I just had to try.'

At 4.10 a.m. on 1 November, 2009 Para managed to speak with an operator known as Cindy from the Rescue Co-ordination Centre. All calls were recorded and transcribed, and the coroner's report included extracts of the conversations that follow. Para is the caller.

Coroner's Report 30/12. Inquest held at Perth Coroners Court 14/09/2012 and 22/10/2012 to 24/10/2012 in the presence of Alastair Neil Hope, State Coroner

CALLER: Yes. We wanting immediately madam. Yes. We are coming to Australia and we have [indistinct] days to go. We are in your country, near the country [indistinct] five hundred kilometres far away, but we don't have food and we don't have water also, but have—there's a huge hole in the bottom of the boat. A lot of water enter into the boat. We want to go immediately to [indistinct], Madam. Can you help me [indistinct]?

CINDY: Okay, you will have to slow down. I am having trouble understanding you. I understand you are …

CALLER: Yes …

CINDY: 500 kilometres from Australia. Do you have a position, a latitude and longitude?

CALLER: Yes. Sorry ma'am [indistinct] Australian [indistinct] but nobody comes here, madam, we are [indistinct] here [indistinct] immediately. Please. I will give licence number [indistinct].

CINDY: Sir, I can't understand you. Slow down. What is your phone number?

CALLER: [indistinct] this number 87 128 [indistinct].

CINDY: Sir, I cannot understand you. Say, again, the phone number.

CALLER: Yes. Okay ma'am. We are waiting for you [indistinct] please immediately. Send that out please ma'am.

CINDY: I cannot help you unless you give me your latitude and longitude. What is your location?

CALLER: Yes.

CINDY: And say it slowly.

CALLER: [indistinct] Okay. Okay.

CINDY: No. Give me your position, sir.

CALLER: Pardon?

CINDY: I need your latitude and longitude, your position. What is the position of your boat?

CALLER: Yes, ma'am [indistinct] to Australia but we have [indistinct] we cannot manage very well, because there's a big hole in bottom of boat. We have a big problem. We cannot go—move one metre, even.

CINDY: Yes, sir. I understand you need assistance, but I need to know where your boat is. What is the nearest point of land?

CALLER: Yes. I already given that [indistinct] number. We want to repeat this number, please [indistinct] madam. Please inform the navy or in person, we want [indistinct].

There was not enough information given to enable the Rescue Co-ordination Centre to determine the boat's location. Para did not know the co-ordinates, but understood they were essential. None of the passengers had been allowed in the cabin, but now Para negotiated with the captain to allow him to go up to look at the instruments and read the figures off the display. The captain also told Para that they were around 500 kilometres from Christmas Island.

Finally, having some details to share, Para tried calling AMSA again, but this time to no avail—by now the battery for the satellite phone was flat. The captain had to start the engine to charge the phone and everyone gathered around Para, fearing the worst.

They continued to bale, sharing the task because after so many days without food or water they were weak and tired. Finally, at 7.14 p.m. Para managed to get through to AMSA on a clearer line and was pleased and relieved to be able to speak with Cindy again.

CINDY: Sir, say again your position.

CALLER: Yes, ma'am. Yes, ma'am, we're here, we're waiting for you here. We have a huge hole in the boat [indistinct].

CINDY: Yes, sir. We …

CALLER: [indistinct]

The Power of Good People

CINDY: We have received your two phone calls, sir, but we need your location. Where are you?

CALLER: [indistinct] another two hours we can manage. There is a lot of water coming into the boat.

For a moment, the line cleared, then Para read out the twelve numbers that meant nothing to him, but so much to the Rescue Co-ordination Centre. RCC staff were able to determine where the stricken boat was, despite limited information, given on a poor and crackly line by someone who had no idea about these matters, so could only give information he thought might be useful, in a language he had not used for many years. They also provided it with an identity: 'Suspected Illegal Entry Vessel (SIEV) 69'.

Para and the other passengers owe their lives to them. To take the garbled information they were given and, in an area spanning some 74 million square kilometres, pinpoint the location of the little boat with accuracy—350 nautical miles north-west of the Cocos Islands—underlines RCC operatives' professionalism and expertise.

'I don't know how they managed to figure out where we were,' Para remarked. 'We were a tiny boat in the middle of a vast ocean, there were no other ships in sight, I was not able to give them much information and my English wasn't good. The satellite connection was terrible and kept dropping out, but somehow they did it. They were amazing.'

In his report, Coroner Alastair Hope complimented RCC on their skills. He remarked: 'In spite of the very limited information provided, RCC operatives were able to identify the location of SIEV 69 with reasonable precision and at 8.02 a.m. a distress broadcast signal was issued.'

No Australian 'assets' were available to help within a realistic distance. The closest vessel was found to be the Taiwanese fishing vessel FV *Kuang Win*, and the master of this ship, Captain Abe, was contacted at 11 a.m. on 1 November. By 12.25 p.m. the *Kuang Win* reported sighting SIEV 69.

The first call from the RCC to the *Kuang Win* was complicated by language issues, so an interpreter was arranged for the second call around 1 p.m.

Then, from across the vast stretches of the Indian Ocean, a huge gas tanker heard the distress call.

During the last thirty years, Para's life, frequently in danger, was saved by strokes of good fortune—just when disaster appeared inevitable, someone or something would appear, as if by divine intervention, and avert the catastrophe. *LNG Pioneer*, a gas tanker from the fleet of the multinational MOL group, was that angel.

The *LNG Pioneer* is huge. Built in 2005, it weighs in at over 93,000 tonnes and 277 metres in length, with the deck more than 17 metres above the sea (the equivalent of a six storey building). Clearly this massive vessel was not physically ideal for an ocean rescue, but on advising RCC that he was about eleven hours' sailing time away, the Master, Captain Brzica, was asked to assist. He immediately altered course and headed towards the stricken little boat. By now, despite the frantic efforts of the balers, seawater was sloshing over the gearbox. No one aboard SIEV 69 knew that help was at hand—they were all trying to think of a plan if the boat sank, which now seemed very likely.

Para recalled that they had spotted the *Kuang Win* around three days before their boat started sinking. It had been difficult to see it during the day because the waves were so huge, but each night they had seen the lights and followed it. On the third day, they were closer and waved T-shirts and shouted to attract its attention. At first, understandably, the *Kuang Win*'s captain feared they may be pirates, so kept his distance, but in time he came close enough to communicate with the crew and asked for an English-speaking person to swim across and come on board.

Everyone had immediately looked to Para, which was reasonable enough—except Para could not swim.

'Come on Para, you have to do this, we are sinking,' they urged. 'You only have to swim a short distance and tell the captain that we need help, then we will all be saved … Everyone can swim; you just have to try.'

So Para jumped into the ocean. And promptly sank.

21
LOST AT SEA

After several minutes of thrashing around in terror, Para caught hold of the rope thrown to him and was dragged back on board, where Sinnathambi helped him.

Seeing this chaos, the captain of the *Kuang Win* was reassured—but not convinced—he was not dealing with pirates, so brought his vessel close enough to communicate by loudhailer. He ordered—with Para, still vomiting seawater, translating—two men to swim to his boat to explain what they were doing.

Two strong swimmers then managed to get to the *Kuang Win* and reassure the captain they were all refugees, not pirates. Then the vessel came close enough to throw across water bottles and some food.

Para, now recovered, shouted to them, pleading for everyone to be taken on the *Kuang Win* as their boat was sinking. But the captain refused, telling them he had been told another big ship—the *LNG Pioneer*—was coming to rescue them. He was concerned that if he took all the refugees on board he would be accused of people smuggling. And he wanted to go fishing. At this point he then ordered the two men off his vessel, leaving them to swim back to their distressed boat, which by now was in very poor shape.

By 5.30 p.m. the RCC operatives were again in contact with the *LNG Pioneer*, which had made good speed. Captain Brzica advised RCC that he was about one nautical mile from SIEV 69, had sighted the sinking vessel and was in communication with the captain of the *Kuang Win*.

In the hours before they arrived at the scene, Captain Brzica and his officers had been holding a risk assessment meeting on the bridge, discussing the possibility that the boat might not have been carrying refugees but was instead planning an attack. In fact, piracy on the high seas is a serious risk—as recently as 2014, according to data from the International Maritime Bureau, pirates took over twenty-one vessels, an increase from twelve the previous year. In addition, four hundred and forty-two sailors were taken hostage. It was a common ploy for pirates to feign they were sinking in order to attract larger ships, then when they were close enough, to swarm aboard the bigger vessel, capturing crew and taking over the ship.

Captain Brzica and his crew had to take this information into account as they sailed towards SIEV 69.

Saving men from a sinking vessel, especially one so small, requires bravery and skill and, in the case of the *LNG Pioneer*, confidence that the parent company will support all actions. Fortunately, the MOL Group takes its responsibilities seriously, which they outline in their CHART.[1]

---

1 CHART: Challenge—Innovate through insight; Honesty—Do the right thing; Accountability—Commit to acting with a sense of ownership; Reliability—Gain the trust of customers; and Teamwork—Build a strong team.

'Organisations often tell us that they have good values,' Para says, 'but then they do something that shows that's only talk. The *Pioneer* showed us that MOL people live by their values. We are so lucky they came.'

Because of its enormous size, the *Pioneer* was not well equipped to mount a sea rescue, but the captain reasonably assumed the much smaller fishing vessel would stay and help. He already had a plan—to use the *Kuang Win* to tow SIEV 69 closer to the *Pioneer*. But by now Captain Abe on the *Kuang Win* was showing signs of impatience.

In a conversation recorded between Captain Abe and RCC a few hours previously (at 1.11 p.m.) and aided by the presence of an interpreter, the RCC's expectations were clearly outlined:

RCC: We request that the Taiwanese fishing vessel remain with the Sri Lankan vessel until the *LNG Pioneer* arrives on scene.

INTERPRETER: When will the *LNG Pioneer* arrive?

RCC: Approximately six hours.

INTERPRETER: If six hours, that's okay because they are only a fishing vessel and cast their nets into the water and need to release some fish, otherwise they will be dragged by the fish.

RCC: If they can stay in the area until *LNG Pioneer* arrives that will be greatly appreciated.

INTERPRETER: Okay, no problem.

At 3.28 p.m. another call took place, again with an interpreter.

INTERPRETER: This gentleman [Captain Abe] says that the boat [SIEV 69] came from Sri Lanka and has been on the journey for twenty-five days and the boat is broken now. This gentleman is now in a situation. His company does not know that he is helping with the other boat and he is worried about the operation of his fishing.

RCC: RCC appreciate the impact on his fishing. We need him to stay there until the *LNG Pioneer* arrives and then he can leave.

INTERPRETER: After it arrives, then can he leave?

RCC: Yes, but only after the *LNG Pioneer* arrives.

RCC: Repeated request to stay until the *LNG Pioneer* arrives; it could be four hours but it could be longer.

INTERPRETER: They rescued two people from the distressed boat. There are two people on their boat. What should they do?

RCC: They should transfer them to the *LNG Pioneer* when it arrives. When *LNG Pioneer* comes on scene it will take charge and then [is] free to leave but cannot leave until *LNG Pioneer* arrives.

INTERPRETER: He was afraid that their boat might be involved in this case because he has not reported this.

At 5.24 p.m. a third call took place, again with an interpreter.

RCC: No change? Good news. If there is any concern, just give us a call, but we are happy for them to talk to each other. I am in contact with the master of the *LNG Pioneer*, so as soon as the passengers have been transferred we will make sure that they can be on their way.

INTERPRETER: What passengers?

RCC: The two passengers on board the fishing vessel we referred to before, so I won't disturb them anymore, but just make sure everyone gets accounted for and they get on board the *LNG Pioneer* and they will be on their way. [The two 'passengers' referred to by RCC had in fact already been ordered by Captain Abe to return to SIEV 69—before swimming back they had asked the *Kuang Win* to rescue everyone, but the captain refused their request.]

It was around this time that the day began unravelling for Para and the others on board SIEV 69— who for two days and nights had been baling for their lives.

At 7.17 p.m. RCC asked the *Kuang Win* to assist with offloading people from SIEV 69 to the *Pioneer*.

INTERPRETER: I need you to clarify—you just need to get the people from the vessel to *LNG Pioneer*?

RCC: No, not to transfer them—need a tow to *LNG*.

INTERPRETER: It is not easy to tow the broken boat; may be hit, may not be able to do. Dangerous.

RCC: What does he expect the 300-metre boat to do? What is he doing?

INTERPRETER: Tried to lead the *LNG* to the small boat; fishing vessel can lead.

RCC: No, no. That vessel cannot manoeuvre safely around small vessels. He needs to get everybody, either with many trips or one trip, and he has to manoeuvre close to the vessel. The vessel cannot manoeuvre, it's too big and too dangerous. It could sink her. So the vessel needs to stay steady and he needs to approach. If it takes ten times, it doesn't matter. He needs to move all those people into the merchant vessel.

INTERPRETER: So just the people, but you said tow the whole boat?

RCC: Whatever he prefers, whatever solution he prefers. If he doesn't feel that it's safe to tow the vessel, then he gets them on board. If he can't get them all at once, he does more than one trip. The mission is to get the people on board safely.

INTERPRETER: They can't leave the boat there?

RCC: I'm not interested in the boat, we are saving lives now and that's what we have to do.

INTERPRETER: Are they refugees?

RCC: Yes. Do the Sri Lankans on board know any English so they can speak to the master?

INTERPRETER: They also have difficulty getting close to the *LNG*, to the big vessel. Also dangerous.

RCC: What is he doing to make sure they get safely on board? What is his plan?

INTERPRETER: He tried to lead the big boat, I don't know his plan [further discussion] … As regarding the two people that they have saved, they have already sent them back to the boat because the *LNG* would get close and save all of them. He has no idea how those people can be rescued. He cannot get close to *LNG* because it is too big.

At 7.37 p.m. Captain Brzica advised RCC that the *Kuang Win* was leaving the scene and moving away. Soon the fishing vessel was out of sight.

Just before sunset, it had disappeared over the horizon. Shortly afterwards, SIEV 69 started sinking quickly.

The little boat that had chugged so steadily from India carrying thirty-nine desperate men and boys, each with a story some would never share, keeled over and quickly sank beneath the waves. For a few minutes, the hull reared up and several men clambered onto it, but then it too disappeared, spilling them into the water, leaving everyone floundering for their lives in an ocean that was now increasingly turbulent.

The passengers grabbed what they could—anything that would float.

Para went under. Luckily one of the men, Ruban, managed to grab Para's shirt and haul him above the waves. 'Swim, Para, swim!' he shouted. 'You can do it, move your arms and legs, keep moving and don't give up.' Then he dragged Para to a couple of discarded diesel tins and forced his hands under the ropes that tied them together.

'Ruban certainly saved my life,' Para recalled. 'People were crying out all around me. It was getting dark and the waves were huge. I have asthma and I could hardly breathe, I was choking on the seawater, and I could only think of Jayantha and Abi as I heard the screams of dying men as they sank beneath the waves. I thought about the two children and the young boy with the birthday cake made of rice. I couldn't see him, but I was sure he would drown. It was really terrible.'

Just on sunset, people from the little boat were seen trying to swim against a big swell towards the *Pioneer*, which was still at least a nautical mile away.

Captain Brzica and his crew watched in horror from the *Pioneer*. They had planned for the *Kuang Win* to either tow SIEV 69 closer, or to take everyone on board the fishing vessel and then transfer them to the tanker.

Desperately, RCC tried to encourage the *Kuang Win* to return to help.

INTERPRETER: They have tried hard. They had stayed there for many hours. If they had seen the boat sinking, they would have rescued the people. They saw the big vessel come and took it to the small boat. They tried to look after their fishing—large amount of money in Taiwan—they have to look after their interests … he is worried about his nets.

RCC: Yes, but there are people in the water drowning.

INTERPRETER: He wants to know if people have been rescued—wants a message they have been rescued.

RCC: We request that he returns to assist with the recovery of people from the water.

INTERPRETER: When he left, the people were safe and after they left the people sank and were in the water. He has to consider his fishnets. He has to balance this. It is hard.

RCC: Tell him there are many people in the water who are drowning and need assistance to be rescued. The big ship cannot rescue the people on their own. If he fails to assist, we will report him and he may be responsible for the drowning.

INTERPRETER: He says that is not reasonable because if they have a big loss what can they say to his company?

RCC: The big ship cannot rescue the people. He is the only other vessel nearby and if he does not assist, the people will die and the authorities will be told that he failed to assist.

INTERPRETER: They are going back now. He said that if they come back to rescue and the company asks them to take the loss, will we talk to the company?

RCC: Yes, we will inform the company that they were responding on our behalf.

INTERPRETER: They are turning back now.

RCC: Thank him and appreciate his assistance. Will pass info to big ship. Please travel back at best speed to rescue people in the water.

INTERPRETER: He is going out for a while but he said he will turn around.

It is eight years since the little fishing boat sank, but the desperation of the RCC operative still resonates.

'I never knew this RCC operator,' Para said, reading the transcripts, 'but I would like to thank him sincerely for persisting with the *Kuang Win*, and for keeping on talking with the Interpreter and trying to persuade Captain Abe to stay and help us. If the *Kuang Win* had stayed, then maybe we would all have survived, but he did not.

'I can't understand why he didn't stay—our boats were so close, he knew we were not pirates, he could see we were sinking. Perhaps he thought we had longer ... I don't know what he was thinking. But when he sailed away from us, we all thought we were doomed. The waves were enormous; it was getting dark. The *Pioneer* was so far away, and so big. We couldn't think how it could rescue us. I knew I couldn't swim, hardly any of us could swim, and the children certainly could not manage.'

The coroner described Captain Abe's actions as 'callous and irresponsible': 'The captain and crew of the FV *Kuang Win* were well aware from the outset that SIEV 69 was a vessel in distress. They had been asked to assist because of concerns that SIEV 69 was likely to sink and on their arrival, they saw persons from SIEV 69 using buckets to bale water out of the boat ... There can be no doubt that when FV *Kuang Win* left the scene SIEV 69 was at risk of sinking at any time. Tragically it did sink within minutes of the FV *Kuang Win* departing.'

So it was against all advice, and despite the desperate pleas, that the *Kuang Win* did leave.

We contacted *LNG Pioneer* crew member Steve Hardie, seven years after the disaster.

'I was particularly disturbed ... with the lack of response and humanity of the operators and crew of the Taiwanese fishing boat prior to, during and post incident,' he observed. 'I now wonder how the master and crew [of the *Kuang Win*] would have felt if the situation was reversed and their ship was sinking and yet a vessel close by did not render all possible assistance; one third of the ship's complement[2] would eventually perish as a result of another vessel's inaction.'

---

2   Steve Hardie is referring here to all the asylum seekers on the fishing boat.

22
HEROES AND VILLAINS

After SIEV 69 sank and Ruban helped Para to get clear, the two men were left clinging to fuel cans, being hurled around the ocean with several others.

'We could see the lights of the huge ship far away in the distance,' Para says. 'I thought we would never be able to reach it because the waves were like mountains and it was almost pitch dark, but Ruban encouraged me.

'Stay with me, Para,' he said. 'I know what I am doing. My family are all fishermen, we lived by the sea and this is why I can swim. I know the night sky; I understand the stars. I am telling you, the sea is our friend and we will survive.'

'The waves were so big and we were thrown up and down so much that we could only see the big ship's lights when we were up in the water, then we would surge down into darkness. It felt like we were not making any headway at all, and the ship sometimes seemed to be getting farther away. Ruban told me he understood currents and he reassured me that we would be saved.

'We could hear people around us calling out. There was one boy I really liked. Kajan had told me that he was studying medicine at Jaffna University, but then he was kidnapped by the army and tortured because they thought he may have helped care for people from the LTTE. His mother paid a big ransom and once he was freed from prison he knew they would come for him again so he travelled to India, trying to find a way to escape. He just wanted to become a doctor and to help people. I liked him and I often spoke with him on the boat—he told me, "People are people, Para. It is my mission to save them. I don't care who they are; it is not for me to judge." He was floating near us, holding onto cans with a few others. We tried to keep together but the waves kept pulling us apart and people just disappeared in the dark water. There were some terrified screams, and I wondered about sharks.

'After a few hours, I heard Kajan calling out desperately. He was cold and tired, and he couldn't hold on to his cans any longer. He begged us to help him, but we couldn't even see him. He sounded so scared. Then there was silence. I could not speak. I cried.

'Suddenly there were just three of us.

'Raja was a young man who had escaped from Sri Lanka at the end of the war. During our voyage, he had told me how he had managed to find a fisherman who took him, his wife and children from the northern tip of Sri Lanka to the Indian coastline, where they had to get into the water and wade ashore. But the Indian Navy had been prepared for the arrival of these refugees, and immediately placed them in massive refugee camps. Raja was allowed to leave the camp each day to work, but his wife and children had to remain inside.

Every day people in the camp were being returned to Sri Lanka, and Raja believed the only way to survive was to try to seek asylum in Australia and then send for his family. Lying on the hot deck, we had shared our plans—we could only talk about our futures as our pasts were too painful to recall.

'Raja was fit and young, but now he was getting tired and started to grab my shirt. Ruban told us to keep apart or we would both drown.'

'What do you know about swimming?' Raja shouted.

'I was in the Sea Tigers and I trained the new recruits,' Ruban replied. 'We used to take them far out in the ocean and make everyone swim back to shore. If they couldn't swim then they learned quickly, or they drowned. Everyone can swim, just keep going.'

'Poor Raja was getting cramps and tiring fast. Ruban kept talking to keep us going. He told us that during the war he once had to abandon his ship and ended up swimming for thirty hours in rough seas before he was found by fishermen close to the shore.

'You just keep going,' he said. 'Look, the big ship is not so far away now. With these tides, I think we can get there in nine hours. I know I can make it. Whether you do or not is up to you.'

'We went on together. 'I looked around and called out for Sinnathambi but it was too dark to see anything, and the currents dragged us this way and that. We tried kicking in the direction of the big ship but the sea was too strong for us. After several hours, I was beginning to feel sleepy—it was so cold. I hadn't heard Raja speak for a long time, then suddenly he called out, "Please find my wife and children, please help them." I looked over to where I heard his voice and saw him, but before I could say anything he held his arms up over his head and simply disappeared. I was shocked, and felt numb. I prayed for him to come up to the surface. But he had gone. Was I next?

'That was when Ruban was really strong for me.

'He said, "Look up at the sky, Para. Do you see those stars? I understand the stars. Look over there, that star tells me it is early evening for your wife and son in India. They think you are safely in Australia; they will be waiting to hear from you. Keep going now so you can call them and tell them you are okay. Look over there at that star ... I know it is the morning in Australia. You will be there soon, and you will have a good job teaching children like you used to. We will both be there very soon."

'And so he talked, all through the night. Sometimes he encouraged me, and other times he shouted at me to keep trying, and not give up. Every now and then we heard another person calling out for help, then silence. It was a truly, truly terrible night.

'Then the stars slowly disappeared and the sky turned grey, then pink. And it was day, and we had survived the long hours of the night. We'd been in the water for maybe ten hours. We looked around and could not see anyone, but ahead of us floated a huge orange ball with ropes on the side. We guessed it had come from the big ship and we managed to paddle to it. We were so weak and numb with cold that it took ages, but somehow, we got there.'

* * *

Captain Brzica had not hesitated—with darkness falling, he immediately activated parachute flares and searchlights and ordered the launching of the starboard lifeboat. At the same time, he tried to regain contact with the *Kuang Win*, which by now was 8 nautical miles away, travelling in a south-easterly direction. There was no response to the calls.

However, by 10 p.m. the fishing vessel had returned to the search area and started working with *Pioneer* to rescue men from the sea. Sadly, for many, Captain Abe's change of heart came too late.

By now the weather had deteriorated so much, with gale force (Beaufort Force 5) winds, high swell and rough seas, that the *LNG Pioneer*'s lifeboat sustained damage and was forced to return. Captain Brzica was aware that he needed to rescue the men in the water, but also protect his own crew members, so he then activated two orange inflatable life rafts, each with a twenty-five-seat capacity. These were tied to the *Pioneer* with long ropes, as were several lifebuoys with self-igniting lights. The captain hoped that any people drifting in the sea could grab the life rafts or buoys and be pulled on board.

His plan worked—every time someone managed to climb on the life raft it was pulled back to the ship and the survivor was hauled on board by a *Pioneer* crew member. It was hard, heavy and dangerous work and the crew worked bravely and tirelessly, dragging out the exhausted men, carrying those who were too weak to climb the ladders. Everyone was immediately given medical care, food and water, and all were able to change into dry clothes, which were generously donated by the crew.

On returning to the scene, the *Kuang Win* stayed for around six hours and rescued eight people from the ocean, subsequently transferring them to the *Pioneer* whose crew managed to rescue nineteen. Twelve people drowned, including the captain and the two young boys. Only one body was recovered from the disaster, and brought to Christmas Island—Tharmeswaran, a primary school teacher.

The operation lasted more than two days.

When Ruban and Para reached the ball, they could see it was a life raft shaped like a small tent. They scrambled in and found three more men huddled inside.

'We all started crying with relief, but then we wondered about the others,' he says. 'Had anyone else survived? The men told me they were very thirsty from swallowing so much seawater, then I found some instructions on the side of the raft that said there was a water bottle and biscuits. We shared the water and we couldn't believe how lucky we were to be alive.

'The floating ball was attached to the big ship, so soon after, they pulled us towards them and finally we were at the bottom of the ladder of the *Pioneer*—up close, we could see how massive it was. Someone from the crew called to us to climb one by one up the moving ladder. Ruban was suddenly hesitant because he thought it could be a Sri Lankan navy ship, but I saw the British flag and told him we were safe to get on it. "How can you be sure?" he asked. "Because I paid attention in school," I replied. He called me a swot and it was the first time we had laughed in a very long time.'

Para was almost right—in fact, *LNG Pioneer* was flying the Bahamas flag, which has the Union Jack on it.

'Somehow, we scrambled unsteadily up the ladders,' he continues, 'and I went last in case I needed to tell the others what to do. It was really hard because we'd been in the ocean for so long that the skin was coming off our hands and we were all so weak. At the top of the ladder a Filipino man took our arms and pulled us on board. "Thank you, thank you," I kept saying, then I asked him, "What day is it?"

'Welcome on board,' he replied. 'It's Thursday, the second of November.'

'That made me stop and think.'

Para struggled for a moment and finally remembered.

'Oh, it's my birthday,' he said. 'I am now thirty-one years old.'

'Congratulations,' my rescuer replied.

'Then he gave us the biggest, most welcoming smile, and we smiled back,' Para says. 'We were safe at last. Later, he gave me his T-shirt. I still have it.'

They were taken to a big cabin and ushered inside. The crew had arranged to have hot air blowing on the survivors because they were all suffering from extreme hypothermia after being in the ocean so long.

'Walking in, to my amazement, I saw around sixteen men from our boat. I was so happy to see them; I could not believe it. We were holding each other, crying and laughing, everyone talking at once, then there was some shouting and we raced out of the cabin and to the side of the ship.

'There came my dear friend Sinnathambi, so exhausted, and swimming so slowly, holding an oil can. "Come on, you can make it!" we called, and he waved an arm and kept going steadily. We lined up along the deck, about seventeen metres above the water. He looked so tired and so small, but he kept going. We were cheering when he reached the bottom of the ladder. Everyone loved this gentle giant of a man. "Grab the ladder, Sinnathambi," we called and he finally caught hold of the trailing rope and slowly started to pull himself up, just as Ruban and I had done.

'We could see how tired he was, and how his feet slipped on the rails, but up he came, smiling his big friendly smile right up at me. Suddenly, about halfway up, his feet slipped from the ropes; his smile turned to alarm as he realised he just did not have the strength to hold on and then he fell, crashing down to the water below. In a second he disappeared, then a few moments later we saw him, cut up by the ship's propellers, clearly dead.

'Everyone fell silent. It was awful. Lovely, kind, generous Sinnathambi—he had come so far with us, he had kept us going when we were scared and losing heart, he had looked after me like a brother, he had shared stories about his wife and daughter, he had shyly told me his dreams for a safe and peaceful life with them. Now nothing was left, just a broken body floating away from the ship. Once again we were reminded that the gods can take away just as easily as they can give.'

Para still dreams about Sinnathambi. 'You are standing in front of your workshop in Australia, rubbing your oily hands on a rag—I see your hand with the two missing fingers, an old injury. You are smiling down at me and telling me that my car is now fixed and running perfectly. I am bringing special foods made by Jayantha for your whole family … we are all safe, and we are happy … our children are playing together ... then I waken and I remember that terrible time, and seeing you—so close to life, but then falling to death.

'Thank you for keeping me safe, Sinnathambi—I wish I could have done the same for you.'

***

Over the course of two days the skilled Captain Brzica and his determined crew rescued nineteen people from the ocean. The *Kuang Win* picked up eight survivors and transferred them to the *LNG Pioneer*. On the third day—after the Australian Rescue Coordination Centre's confirmation of seawater temperatures and the impossibility of survival—the search and rescue mission was called off.

We contacted Captain Brzica seven years after the tragedy. 'I can clearly remember Para, who was the sole English speaker among the group and helped us immensely with communicating concerns of the rescued asylum seekers,' he said.

'He showed immense courage and determination even after the ordeal that befell him and his fellow survivors. His friendly attitude and enthusiasm towards life even rubbed on to his fellow survivors, giving them something to be cheerful about in such drastic conditions. He informed me of how he was kidnapped twice by the Sri Lankan authorities during the war and released against ransom, which his brother managed to pay. How he and others planned and decided to bid adieu to their families and everything back home and embark on a small dinghy towards a safer future.'

Captain Brzica continued, 'Memories [of the event] brought back indescribable emotions I went through during the course of the rescue, both during and later.

'It was on November 1st 2009 on her voyage from Hazira, India to Dampier Whitnell Bay in Australia that *LNG Pioneer* received a relayed distress call from the Australian Rescue Co-ordination Centre in Canberra to assist with a distressed refugee vessel.

'We were initially advised of 40 personnel being in distress on a dinghy some 350 nautical miles off the remotely located Cocos Islands, west of the Australian Coast. Our own vessel was about 120 nautical miles from the distressed position. We immediately proceeded at full speed to rendezvous with the distressed craft. When within VHF range, we established contact with the Taiwanese deep-sea fishing vessel [the *Kuang Win*] which was at sight before us, and we also tried to establish contact with the distressed craft. As soon as we arrived at the site the fishing boat departed, switching off all communications equipment.

'Unfortunately, by the time we arrived just before sunset and were about one nautical mile from the craft, it suddenly started sinking. Initially its freeboard [distance from waterline to continuous deck] decreased and later sank stern first. At this time, we could still see people hanging from the bow of the boat, trying to stay afloat, but we could not sight any flotation aids. Finally, the entire boat went in the water, leaving behind its whirl trail of oil and several dim figures trying to stay afloat by splashing their hands frantically.

'It was a sorry sight for us, but effective actions needed to be taken without wasting time if we wanted maximum survivors; at the same time all crew and officers on *LNG Pioneer* needed to have their morals and wits to be in right frame of mind, having never encountered such a situation ever before in their seafaring lives—or otherwise.'

Captain Brzica described the lifeboats being prepared to be lowered, but then finding it unsafe to remain in the sea in such inclement weather, even with lights, so the starboard boat that was in the waves was recalled—but not before sustaining slight damage.

'After this we needed to think quickly and alternative arrangements had to be made for rescue without risking the lives of our own officers and crew,' he said. 'Two of our twenty-five-capacity life rafts were activated and dropped in the sea, tied to the vessel by rope along with several lifebuoys with self-igniting lights. This was to ensure that any person drifting by could get hold of the life raft or lifebuoys and could be pulled on board to safety.

'Whenever we saw any survivor boarding the life raft, it was pulled back to our vessel and using pilot ladders and gangways we managed to haul these people on board ... then they were taken to a designated area on the ship and after medical treatment were given water and food.

'In this way, over the course of two days we rescued nineteen people from the water. It was only on the third day—after the Australian RCC's confirmation of seawater temperatures and the impossibility of survivability—that the Search and Rescue mission was called off.

'The Taiwanese fishing vessel had rescued another eight survivors, the last one was afloat in the water for eighteen hours and had drifted some 22 nautical miles. If the fishing vessel [the *Kuang Win*] had stayed for a bit longer [at the beginning], then more survivors could have been rescued immediately. But no one could have predicted the dinghy would have sunk so quickly. Unfortunately, one of those people delivered by the *Kuang Win* was deceased. The mood on board was sombre as we cleared the meat room and placed the body in there. When we learned the deceased was the father of a teenager we had rescued, we could not bear to inform him until we reached port.

'After the rescue, the survivors were split into two groups. One group was placed in the Suez Crew cabin and the second group in the Engine Changing Locker cabin. Both areas were chosen for the availability of bathroom facilities—the idea was not isolation but providing better care with a dedicated ship's crew helping with requirements from food to just talking.

'We finally headed for Christmas Island in Australia, where we were met by the Australian authorities, including Police and Immigration. As well, our General Manager Andy Hill arrived from the UK. Detectives interviewed all our crew members, and again two weeks later when the *LNG Pioneer* arrived at Whitnell Bay. We arranged counselling for members of our crew.

'The meat room was fumigated and cleaned, but after the incident a new issue arose,' Captain Brzica continued. 'Our crew consisted mainly of Filipinos, who can be quite religious, with beliefs in supernatural powers.

'After we had departed from Christmas Island one of the cooks came to me and declared he had come across the ghost of the dead person inside the meat room. Although to some people this can sound absurd, it can actually turn things upside down when you are working in a close environment like a ship. And the cooks often had to access the provision chambers more than three times a day. The cooks insisted they could only access the area in groups of four—I realised we had to treat their concerns seriously and do something about them. Fortunately, our General Manager, Andy Hill, was sailing with us so after consultation with him we decided to bring in a priest when we arrived at our destination. On arriving at Dampier, a priest was invited who blessed the vessel and conducted a Mass for the crew. After this the situation normalised.

'This was the part of the entire rescue operation which I still believe was the toughest, as you cannot deal with something which is not there in the first place, but has crept up from fears in the human mind. We had the option of a psychologist or a priest. We chose the latter and it worked.'

Para hopes to be able to meet with Captain Brzica and some of the *Pioneer*'s crew members one day. 'Years later, when I saw the photos of our tiny boat in that enormous ocean, I could not believe that we had survived. So many terrible things happened during those hours,' he says. 'People I had come to know well died in front of me. Some drowned, some were taken by sharks. But many were saved. Without the *Pioneer*, all of us would probably have died.'

Summing up the event, and the company's philosophies, Andy Hill, General Manager, observed, 'You may find us just a little humble and matter of fact in our discussions on this event. Whilst saving life at sea is a legal obligation on a Master, we learn at an early age to respect the sea itself … we look out for and look after each other regardless of our origins, faith or beliefs. It is what we do. We go about it daily and without accolade, and neither do we seek it.

'Behind us we have a team of professionals that provide the daily support, guidance and services needed to keep our ships at sea, our crews motivated and our customers happy. I would particularly like to mention our Principals, Mitsui OSK Lines, and the Australian Maritime Safety Authority, without whose support we could not have achieved what we did and saved all we could.'

Thanks to the persistence of AMSA operators, the skills of Captain Brzica and his brave crew on *LNG Pioneer*, the help from Captain Abe—who did after all eventually return to the scene—Para and many of those on the boat survived.

But thirteen died in their attempt to reach Australia.

23

WELCOME TO AUSTRALIA

Safely aboard the *LNG Pioneer*, Para and his fellow survivors were well cared for. Climbing on board with nothing except the clothes they were wearing when their boat sank, they were soon overwhelmed by the crew's generosity as shorts and T-shirts were donated, along with shoes. Crew members moved from their cabins, allowing the men to squeeze in together. They ended up a few bunks short, so the crew provided mattresses to make the survivors all comfortable.

They had to remain in their cabins, but food was provided and they were finally able to relax and feel safe.

'The food was wonderful,' Para says. 'We were all so hungry, after almost a month with just rice water. The chefs made us soup and we ate lots of seafood. The fish was so fresh, and the crew were all so generous and kind. Of course, we were terribly sad that so many had died. And we were all traumatised by the journey and the sinking of the other boat, as well as our little boat, and spending so long in the ocean, thinking we were about to die. But everyone on the *Pioneer* really looked after us, and it certainly helped. I will never forget their kindness.'

After about three days of sailing they were told they had reached Christmas Island, but the tanker was so huge it had to moor offshore. Soon members of the Australian Federal Police arrived and told the men to gather their possessions and hand over any belongings for safekeeping.

'It didn't take long because most of us had absolutely nothing,' Para says, 'but some people had managed to keep their passports and papers in plastic bags, tucked in their underwear. They had done this so that if they drowned and washed up on a beach somewhere, people would be able to identify their bodies. I had lost everything in the ocean. The police were thorough—they took everything and even emptied and took away the contents of the rubbish bins. At that stage I think they were trying to identify one among us as being the people smuggler. But the only one who could have helped them was the young captain, and he had drowned.'

They were taken down several decks and found Captain Brzica and his crew all lined up, waiting to say goodbye.

'We shook hands with everyone, and the captain hugged me. He said, "I wish you well, Para. In the future life may be hard, and it may take a long time before everything works out, but you have survived a difficult test—perhaps the greatest test of your life—and I hope you will continue to manage. Take care."

'I tried to thank him—but how can you adequately thank someone who has saved your life? I would love to speak with him properly, now that my English has improved.

'Then we disembarked through the side of the ship, where we were given lifejackets before climbing aboard an open vessel. None of us liked being out in a small boat on the ocean again, but this vessel was so much better than our old one. We had to sit close together on the deck, and were ferried to the island. Once we'd tied up alongside the wharf we climbed the steps and when we were all gathered at the top a policeman called out, "Welcome to Australia".

'I honestly thought this was the end of my difficulties— I thought, We did it, we're safe. And I sent a prayer of thanks to God, believing this was the end of my troubles.

'How innocent I was.'

* * *

The men were all taken for health checks. Amazingly, there were few physical injuries. Thanks to the crew on the *Pioneer*, everyone had been able to rest and recover from their ordeal on the journey and in the ocean.

The men were asked their names and other basic questions during several initial interviews, then they were assigned to the different camps. Para had been asked to look after Anojan, the nineteen-year-old boy whose father had drowned when their boat sank, so they were both placed in the family camp.

Once there, Para had something he must do right away ... phone home.

'We lined up near the phones in the detention centre,' he said. 'Some of us had lost everything in the ocean including our notebooks. Luckily, I could easily remember the two most important numbers—Jayantha's and my mum's. It felt like a lifetime since I had last spoken with them. I wondered if Jayantha was okay, and how Abi was. Had they heard that we were safe, or did they think we had all drowned? And what about them? Were they okay? We had been away for so long with no news. I suddenly felt very scared—what if something had happened to them?

'Finally, it was my turn. I pressed Jayantha's number into the phone. My hands were shaking so much I could barely manage, and then I heard it ringing, and ringing. I did not know that she was sitting at the temple with Abi, praying for me.'

* * *

Jayantha had heard nothing from Para since he left on the train over thirty days beforehand. Then at the beginning of November the agent had phoned to tell her that Para's boat had sunk in the middle of the Indian Ocean, with no survivors. People all over Chennai were talking about the tragedy, as many thought they knew someone who had relatives or friends on that boat.

Jayantha became more frightened as time went on. What should she do now? Who would help her? Here she was, living alone in a foreign country with a two-year-old son. She had no income, no family support and few friends. Those friends she did have were so poor themselves that they could not support her and Abi. Welfare did not exist. Jayantha had been managing by living frugally and pawning her jewellery. When she was told that Para's boat had sunk, she was down to her last two bangles. She decided to cope by making a plan.

'I was distraught, but I had to keep calm for Abi,' she says. 'I knew we would not be able to survive alone in India for much longer, and I thought the only way was to plan to end our lives.

'I decided to wait for thirty days, and if there was no more news, then I would believe that Para had died, and I would make sure that Abi was also dead before killing myself. I had to be sure Abi did not end up begging on the streets without me. It all seemed perfectly sensible at the time. I had two gold bangles left. If I sold one, I could manage for the thirty days, and then I would write a note and wrap it around the last bangle so that people would know who we were, why we had died, and be able to afford to bury us. It was easy enough to buy poison ... I could not bear to contemplate killing Abi and myself, but it was the only solution. In the meantime, I could only hope and pray.'

From the moment Para left, Jayantha had been visiting the temple each day to pray for his safety, and she told her story to a priest who tried to keep her hopes up. The priest knew them all, as Para used to visit the temple each week on his way to his painting job, and he had grown fond of Para, Jayantha and their baby son. Whenever Jayantha went to the temple, the priest would talk to her and pray with her for Para's safety.

Not long before Jayantha found out Para had survived, the priest came across Jayantha holding Abi tightly and weeping. With a deep sigh, Jayantha told him she had been told that the boat was definitely lost, with everyone on board, but that she felt in her heart that somehow Para was still alive.

The priest then took three flowers and held them in his hand.

'Look,' he said, 'I am going to cast these flowers in the air. If they land upside down, then sadly it means your husband has died. But if they land with their faces to the sun, then he is surely alive and safe.'

Then he took the small red flowers and tossed them in the air. All three landed with their petals facing upwards. Jayantha dared to hope.

Five days later, there was still no news, and Jayantha was still hoping, even though Para's brother Panneer had called to tell her that he had spoken with their cousin, who believed the boat was lost. His parents were preparing a funeral service for Para at their home near Jaffna. With only twenty days left before her savings ran out, Jayantha was having to think seriously about her plan.

The temple had closed for the day, but Jayantha was still sitting in the entrance with Abi, warmed by the evening sun. By now, she thought, everyone was sure that Para had died. There had been no news for so long, and how could such a small boat have possibly made that incredible journey? What a shame that so many young men had died trying to find safety. Would she be able to carry out her plan if Para really had died, as they all believed?

Fearing the worst, but refusing to give up hope, Jayantha took Abi's chubby little hand in hers. She placed three flowers in his palm.

'Throw them in the air, Abi—let's both pray for Appi.'

Abi smiled and tossed the flowers. They spun swiftly, caught on the warm evening breeze, before landing on the dusty ground ... each one facing upwards.

The Power of Good People

Moments later, Jayantha's phone rang. Someone was calling her from Australia's Christmas Island Detention Centre.

* * *

Leaving the temple, the priest caught sight of Jayantha and Abi, both crying softly. Fearing the worst, he hurried across the courtyard, then slowed down in relief when he realised these were tears of joy. Jayantha told him that she had just spoken with Para, and that he was safe.

'I told you, I told you,' the priest repeated, smiling broadly. 'Shiva was looking after your husband. I knew he would be safe.'

Back at the phone booth, thousands of kilometres away, Para carefully replaced the phone and looked up to see the Australian immigration officer was also crying.

'May I make one more call, to my mum?'

'Of course you can; here's a phonecard.'

This time, as the phone rang in Jaffna, Para hoped the news would not be too much for his mother. Jayantha had just told him that everyone had believed for many days that he was dead, and his mother was grief-stricken. What would he find?

* * *

In the northern tip of war-ravaged Sri Lanka, just outside the small village of Alaveddy, Para's mother touched a large framed photograph of her son.

She remembered battling through the storm to reach the hospital on the day of his birth, then holding the newborn, marvelling at his perfect features, and she wept.

This long war had left Tamils decimated and displaced, with no hope of a land to call their own. So many innocent people had died—Tamils and Sinhalese alike. People around the world didn't seem to know about the atrocities of the war's final days, about thousands of ordinary families slaughtered as they tried to shelter where they had been driven. This war had raged for almost the entire life of her children, had killed her brother, her nieces and nephews ... so many family members. And it had taken away her oldest son Panneer to England, and her daughter Pugalini to Switzerland. At least they were both safe, but so far away. How could she live with this latest news about Para?

Shoulders shaking, she draped the funeral wreath of chrysanthemums around the photograph. This, and her memories, were all she had left of her son.

Family and friends were gathered quietly in the adjoining room. Para's university friends had arrived; cousins, aunties and uncles had come from great distances. People were starting to reminisce about the young man who had seemed invincible. Later, long after the event, each one shared with Para what they were thinking.

Uncle Jegarasa remembered the day young Para had taken fruit from his orchard and received a massive beating for it. Then he had felt guilty when he realised the fruit was for Para's beloved grandmother.

Uncle Ganesh could only recall how hard Para had worked when he was living with him and how he had loved and looked out for his young cousin Kuddi, who had later died in an airstrike.

Uncle Kunam remembered the earnest young man who had arrived in the middle of the night following their displacement, carefully looking after his elderly grandmother and young sister and never complaining about the interruption to his studies, or the lack of food, or the terrible weather.

His dad was thinking about the day he had beaten Para for watching *Tarzan* on the shared television in the village, and how his son would patiently read all the political pages to him from the newspaper.

The reminiscences brought fleeting smiles and more tears.

Everyone had special memories of a loving, determined, clever and compassionate young man.

Para's mother was thinking of how devastated he was on the day they had to leave their dog Tiger behind. Then she remembered Para's devoted grandmother, her own mother. Then she recalled the time when she was laid up with influenza—they had no food or money—and Para had gone out, found a fallen coconut, cleaned and shelled it, and exchanged it for sugar. Then, intent on making some money for food for them all, he searched the village to find many more coconuts, muddied from lying where the wind had hurled them. She remembered the fierce determination of the little boy as he cut and scraped the rough shells. She sighed and touched the garland again, fussing with it as if Para was there, wearing it.

A shroud of grief blanketed the little house.

It was eleven o'clock. The phone rang—that would be Panneer calling from England. She quickly answered it.

'Panneer, this is too sad,' she said, sobbing. 'We are holding a funeral, but we don't even have a body. Your brother is lost in the ocean; my heart is breaking ... have you heard from your sister today?'

'Mum? It's not Panneer, it's me, Para. I'm safe.'

'No, Para is lost in the ocean. Para has died. We are having a funeral right now.'

'Mum, it's me. Honestly. I'm your son, Para. I'm safe. I'm in Australia. I have just spoken with Jayantha. Don't cry, Mum, I am safe. Please, call Panneer and Pugalini to let them know.'

'But we are having a funeral for you! Everyone is here—your father and uncles and cousins and friends from university. Your teachers and some people I don't even know. We have your photo here, and the garland. What shall I tell everyone?'

'Oh Mum, please tell everyone hello from me. I'm okay, I'm safe. And tell them I'm sorry for the trouble. I'll write to you and explain everything ...

'... and Mum, please tell everyone ... *nanri*.'

PART III

24

THE UNFINISHED STORY

It's Tuesday 1st August 2017. I sit on the beach in Apollo Bay with Para. Seven and a half years have passed since he slipped out of India on a tiny, unseaworthy vessel to an uncertain future—but with hope in his heart.

Today the sea is a brilliant blue; little waves, tipped with white foam, break gently to the shore. It is one of those midwinter, magical, good-to-be-alive days. In the distance, we see yachts from the sailing club, their sails puffed by the capricious breeze, and much farther out a huge container ship slowly makes its way across the horizon. We don't speak. There is nothing to say.

Para is here, but Jayantha and Abi are not.

In 2011 Para was released from nearly two years in detention and later granted a Permanent Resident visa. As soon as he was permitted to seek employment, he took every job he could find. He cleaned homes, factories, kitchens and hotels. The work was heavy but he was determined to earn money to send back to Jayantha and his parents—and to save to repay his brother and sister.

In 2013, he began work as a cultural adviser in Nauru Immigrant Detention Centre, but had to leave after two years when he discovered that he had to be living in Australia for the time to count towards applying for his citizenship. He then worked for Diversitat, a community service organisation that supports culturally and linguistically diverse communities, interpreting and helping clients with welfare issues.

In 2015, with much-improved English, he obtained a job at Geelong's University Hospital, where he works in the Intensive Care Unit on the support team. He also gained a certificate in Aged Care and has been working night shifts in an aged care home, where he overcame initial prejudice to be the most popular attendant—now residents particularly ask for him.

Wherever he works, he soon becomes a valued team member and leader. He is extremely popular and has a wide network of friends from around the world. Presented with an opportunity, he will seize it and make the very best of life.

Everyone around Para sees him as an inspiring example of a refugee integrating happily into Australian life, making a positive contribution.

But Para is still separated from Jayantha.

'Every day I go to work, I talk to people, I smile. But inside, my heart is breaking,' he says.

Abi was a baby when Para left; he is now ten years old. Para has been absent for seven of Abi's birthdays.

'It breaks my heart that they are still not here with me—how can I ever make it up to them?'

How indeed. Para has applied for every possible visa for Jayantha—a Special Humanitarian Visa and a Partner Visa.

The first application was refused when the government

changed the law that enabled refugees to sponsor their spouse and children on a humanitarian visa. This was back in 2013 in response to the deep concerns among some parts of the Australian population about the increase in boat arrivals. The dangers from which so many people were trying to escape seemed to have been discounted in favour of appeasing the electorate.

So they then applied for a Partner Subclass 309 visa.

In 2013, with this next application well underway, Jayantha received the following letter from the Department of Immigration:

> I am writing to you about changes to processing of Family Migration visa applications sponsored by people who arrived in Australia as illegal maritime arrivals (IMAs).
>
> Your visa application has been identified as being affected by a new instruction ('Direction 62') by the Minister for Immigration and Border Protection. This instruction states that Family Migration visa applications sponsored by IMAs will henceforth be given the lowest processing priority.
>
> As your sponsor arrived in Australia as an IMA and is not an Australian citizen your application will not be processed until all applications of higher priority have been finalised. As a result, your visa application will not be able to be processed for many years. There is no priority for families sponsored by an IMA who are facing compelling or compassionate circumstances.
>
> Applicants who have already lodged valid applications and have paid the Visa Application Charge (VAC) will not be refunded the VAC even if they withdraw their application. We recommend that you cancel any travel plans, and cancel any

appointments for health, DNA and character checks, if these have been arranged.

As this visa processing instruction has been made by the Minister for Immigration and Border Protection, this office is unable to assist with further enquiries and complaints about this change.

If your sponsor becomes an Australian citizen, please advise this office.

Their despair was profound. We worried for their welfare. But resilient as ever, they saw the chink of light in the last sentence and took the next opportunity. On Australia Day, 26 January, 2017, Para became a proud Australian citizen and was able to send this new information to Immigration. As an Australian citizen, rather than just a refugee who arrived by boat, he was no longer disadvantaged in his application to sponsor his wife and son to Australia.

They were so nearly here! Para was looking at schools for Abi—an ecstatic reunion was planned.

But now the Australian High Commission in Colombo has asked for yet more documents—a number of which had already been previously supplied, and some which are unobtainable.

And so it goes on. Para and Jayantha are asked for certificates and documents; they supply them, then a few days or weeks later there are more documents required. Para fears it will never end.

I watch as he lets the sand trickle between his fingers and wonder if he feels their lives are also just slipping away. He turns to me.

The Power of Good People

'Mum, writing the book was wonderful, it helped me to remember and thank all the good people. But now I wonder, where have the good people gone?'

Jayantha is a mother separated from her husband for far too long. They should have shared their son's milestones, his birthdays and his achievements at school, but instead Jayantha is travelling the road of a single young mother. And living where she does, this is particularly hard. Close to despair, Para frequently wonders, What more can the Department of Immigration want from us? Why are they delaying our application? I am breaking my promise to Jayantha.

Looking far out to sea, immersed in thought, Para sighs deeply. I ask him what he is thinking. I think along the lines of anger, desperation and frustration.

After another long silence, he replies. And once again, exactly as I did six years ago, I have underestimated him.

'You know, we decided to write the book,' he says, 'and then if it's successful and makes some money, we want to donate to a charity? Well, now it's nearly finished I have been thinking and talking with Jayantha and we want to send the money to orphanages in Sri Lanka—especially in the war-torn Vanni area.

'A friend of ours runs a charity, and in the past Jayantha and I have given as much money as we could afford to help them. He recently helped a war-affected family to buy chickens and cows to help with their daily needs. He is a good man and I know all the money we send will be spent on children, widows and older people whose families were all killed in the war. We may not make much money from the book, but whatever we manage, let's spend it in the right way. I promised to help them—let's do that.'

The unfinished story

Postscript

Wednesday 30th August 2017

Our book is finished. Our long-suffering, incredibly professional and infinitely patient publisher, Cathi Lewis, has helped us so much along this journey to bring to light a story that so needed to be told—and now we have a book!

'No more corrections, no time for additions,' she says. 'Time for the typesetter; amendments at your peril,' she says.

So how can I tell her that we have a final paragraph that must be included?

I call her to share news we have longed for since 2010. The Department of Immigration and Border Protection has just written to Jayantha:

'I wish to advise that a decision has been made on this application and a visa has been granted on 30th August 2017.'

Can it be true? To make sure, we call our equally tenacious immigration lawyer, Kerry. He responds with an email,

'Now your life in Australia can truly begin as a family.'

The phones start to ring. Everyone is delighted. We tell Cathi that we have an extra paragraph and explain the latest development. Her reply:

'Congratulations to you all for your work and patience and your prayers, and waiting and waiting and waiting … we are so thrilled … let me know when Jayantha and Abi are finally flying into Melbourne.'

We reflect one last time on the title of our book—'The Power of Good People'.

Yes, good people are powerful, let us always remember this.

EPILOGUE

Sri Lanka's Civil War was long, hard and terrible in every way. No good has come of it and far too many good people, Sinhalese and Tamil alike, suffered greatly because of it.

If only the words of the Tamil philosopher and poet Kaniyan Pungundranar's 'Purananuru' had been heeded:

> To us all towns are one, all men our kin ...
> We marvel not at the greatness of the great;
> Still less despise we men of low estate.

Sri Lanka was my home; it is a beautiful island with a gentle climate, lush scenery and perfect beaches, but the underside is terribly dark, with appalling torture and abuse. And the worst thing is, most governments around the world know, yet refuse to act to stop it.

Unstopped is a report released in July 2017 by the International Truth and Justice Project (ITJP). It shows why Sri Lanka is not safe for Tamils, explaining that in 2016/17 'both the military and police in Sri Lanka continue to abduct, unlawfully detain, rape and torture Tamils'.

In the report's foreword, Yasmin Sooka observes, 'The conflict has not ended for many Tamils in Sri Lanka and is still being perpetrated through unlawful abductions, detention and torture. Witnesses describe being tortured and raped by the security forces, some as recently as 2017. What is shocking is the high number of victims … who have been tortured not once but on multiple occasions—in one case as many as five times.' The report is terrible to read. In meticulous detail it describes the abductions, the prison cells and the various types of torture which included severe beatings, burnings, near-drownings and multiple rapes.

Following a four-day visit to Sri Lanka in July 2017, Ben Emmerson, the UN Special Rapporteur on Human Rights and Counter Terrorism, concluded that torture under the present government remains 'endemic and routine'. Emmerson noted:

> Torture of those in custody under the PTA is on an "industrial scale" and is among the worst in the world… There have been many statements of good intention, but so far little in the way of effective action to bring about a lasting and just settlement to the conflict. It seems that some small steps are now, at last being taken, in that direction. My plea to the Government and the people of Sri Lanka is to let these be the right steps, and not to allow the process to be diverted by retrograde elements in the security establishment and their allies in Government.

The Power of Good People

I experienced torture firsthand; my heart breaks when I think of those people still subjected to it and I am determined to do everything in my power to help them.

Tamils were severely affected by the war; they are still being kept in refugee camps and their lands are occupied by the military. Many Tamils still don't have proper houses. Tamil children who were disabled in the war don't have proper facilities to study. Eighty thousand widows are living with their children and thousands of children are orphans.

I implore the international community to intervene in the war crimes inquiry to bring justice for Tamils. And to urge the Sri Lankan government to stop Sinhala colonisation of Tamil land.

Asylum seekers are people who for some reason were forcibly displaced from their homes. They may have had to leave their loved ones and they all need a safe place to live peacefully with their family. They have many stories to tell. You can make a difference in their life, just like Alison and her family—who changed my life—and her friends. Help just one refugee, and you will be making a difference in the world.

Many people have experienced similar hardships and problems to mine, and there are many more whose lives have been much worse. All of us have one thing in common—we have survived only through acts of kindness and compassion, and the power of good people.

I wanted to share my stories as a way of reaching out to all those people who have helped me in some way, to demonstrate

Epilogue

that often a simple act of kindness can make a profound difference to someone's life.

To each of you I say *nanri*—thank you—from my heart.

If there is righteousness in the heart, there will be beauty in the character.
If there is beauty in the character, there will be harmony in the home.
If there is harmony in the home there will be order in the nations.
When there is order in the nations, there will be peace in the world.

Confucius.

Nanri—நன்றி—Thank you

The Purananuru

'The Purananuru' is a popular Tamil poetical work. A treatise on kingship, it explores what a king should be, how he should act, how he should treat his subjects and how he should show his generosity. Containing four hundred poems of varying length, composed by more than one hundred and fifty poets, the poems deal with such matters as war, politics and wealth, as well as aspects of everyday living.

The poem below comes from the Purananuru; it is Para's favourite.

> To us all towns are one, all men our kin,
> Life's good comes not from others' gifts, nor ill,
> Man's pains and pain's relief are from within,
> Death's no new thing, nor do our bosoms thrill
> When joyous life seems like a luscious draught.
> When grieved, we patient suffer; for, we deem
> This much-praised life of ours a fragile raft
> Borne down the waters of some mountain stream
> That o'er huge boulders roaring seeks the plain
> Tho' storms with lightning's flash from darkened skies.
> Descend, the raft goes on as fates ordain.
> Thus have we seen in visions of the wise!
> We marvel not at the greatness of the great;
> Still less despise we men of low estate.
>
> *Kaniyan Pungundranar,* Puranuru, *192*
> *(Translated by GU Pope, 1906)*

MEMORIAL SPEECH

Given by Para Paheer at the memorial service at the Christmas Island Detention Centre for those who drowned on the journey to Australia

Today, we are joining together to remember our friends who died.

On 1st of November 2009—just one year ago, when we were travelling to Australia, our vessel sank in the ocean 350 nautical miles northwest of the Cocos islands.

In this tragic incident, we lost twelve people. Today we remember them. I am Para, one of the survivors of the tragedy, and I would like to share their stories.

We are Sri Lankan Tamils. Because of the war that was happening in our country, we couldn't continue to live there. We feared we would be abducted, tortured and killed and we were constantly threatened.

We fled from our country, we started our travelling on 11th October 2009 to seek asylum in Australia. We had been told we would be transferred to a large vessel after a few days sailing but after ten days at sea, we realised we had been deceived.

After 27 days afloat, our vessel developed a leak and in spite of all our efforts to stop the water we could not keep the boat afloat, and it started to sink.

Group by group we tried to remove the water. We worked hard. Then one of the crew gave me his phone to contact the Australian navy emergency service and Australian Red Cross. They told us that because the waves were so rough they could not help us at once, but they would send a ship to help us.

Nine hours later a fishing boat appeared we waved towards it, it came near us we explained our situation then the boat captain said that the Australian government was sending a ship. At around 6.30 pm we saw a ship in the distance coming towards us. Unfortunately, before the ship came near us our vessel sank. Most of us on board the boat were unable to swim

I saw that some of us were swimming towards the ship others were in the water, shouting for help. In front of me three people drowned. I was in the water for 8 hours until I managed to reach the ship on 2nd November. I cannot forget this day because 2nd November is my birthday. I think I was reborn in the world.

We will never forget our people. Every day at night we see them and they are shouting 'Please help us'. But we cannot help them. On that day twelve people drowned, and twenty-seven survived.

Unfortunately, because we came from different parts of Sri Lanka, we did not know each other. I wonder, who were they? where are their families? We only know their nicknames, but we also know that they each had a heart of gold, they loved life, they loved their families, they died seeking freedom from oppression.

Their smiles would light up a room and I can tell you all, they have died, but they are right here in our hearts. And I am sure in the hearts of their dear families and friends.

You are great and I want to thank you for your care and support … and for your love.

Memorial speech

I say thank you to our priest, sister and the community of Christmas Island; to the officers of the Department of Immigration and Serco.

So, thank you for being here. For sharing the memory of our people. For remembering them so dearly.

And let me finish this by saying to the twelve who died:

To each and every one of you, every day we will remember you, and we will love you forever.

Thank you.

REFERENCES

When I embarked upon writing *The Power of Good People* with Para, I realised the author's weighty responsibility to produce an honest and accurate narrative. An enormous amount of research has gone into the book; links were followed and histories and accounts carefully read. In addition to the historical and analytical literature, I yearned to learn more about the social history and culture of this embattled country and its brave people. These are a selection of the many books and references I found utterly engaging and completely unforgettable.

Books

Anuk Arudpragasam, *The Story of a Brief Marriage*, Flatiron Books, 2016

Commodore Ajith Boyagoda, *A Long Watch: War, captivity and return in Sri Lanka*, Hurst & Company, 2016

Trevor Grant, *Sri Lanka's Secrets: How the Rajapaksa regime gets away with murder*, Monash University Publishing, 2014

Frances Harrison, *Still Counting the Dead: Survivors of Sri Lanka's hidden war*, Portobello Books, 2012

Rohini Mohan, *The Seasons of Trouble: Life amid the ruins of Sri Lanka's civil war*, Verso Books, 2014

Rajith Savanadasa, *Ruins*, Hachette Australia, 2016

Shyam Selvadurai, *The Hungry Ghosts*, Telegram, 2014

Samanth Subramanian, *This Divided Island: Stories from the Sri Lankan war*, Penguin Books 2014, Atlantic Books 2015

Roma Tearne, *Mosquito*, Harper Press, 2010

Gordon Weiss, *The Cage: The fight for Sri Lanka and the last days of the Tamil Tigers*, The Bodley Head, 2011

References

Online

International Truth and Justice Project, *Unstopped: State Torture and Sexual Violence in 2016/17*, <http://www.itjpsl.com/reports/unstopped#english>

Tamil Guardian, <http://www.tamilguardian.com>

TamilNet, <https://www.tamilnet.com>

United Nations in Sri Lanka, 'Full statement by Ben Emmerson, UN Special Rapporteur on Human Rights and Counter Terrorism, at the conclusion of his official visit', <https://lk.one.un.org/news/full-statement-by-ben-emmerson-un-special-rapporteur-on-human-rights-and-counter-terrorism-at-the-conclusion-of-his-official-visit>, 14 July 2017

www.ingramcontent.com/pod-product-compliance
Lightning Source LLC
Chambersburg PA
CBHW071857290426
44110CB00013B/1186